THE LIFE OF AN UNKNOWN AUTHOR

The Life of an Unknown Author

*An Anthology on Writing and Publishing
from Some of the Best Authors You Haven't Yet Read*

*Edited by
Jodi Cowles, Rachael Mitchell, and Leslee Stewart
Founders of The Unknown Authors Club*

the
UNKNOWN
authors club

We dedicate this book to
the unfamous, unpublished, unknown authors everywhere:

We see you. We are you. We welcome you.
Your words and your stories matter.
So, keep writing.

Together we rise.

"Do not despise these small beginnings,
for the Lord rejoices to see the work begin."
Zechariah 4:10

Sometimes you have to create what you want to be part of.

Howard Schultz

Contents

Foreword

When I started the Punchline Writing Cohorts it was because I was in a season of my life, as a literary agent, where I couldn't represent every author I liked or got excited about. I had, and still have, two small children and currently reside in France, which is approximately forty-two time zones away from most of the authors that send me their book proposals.

Since working with an author is a multiple-year journey, I am trying to practice the wisdom of my own mother, who has always said to "not lose your peace" from saying "yes" to too many things. However, I know a lot about the publishing industry. I know what agents and publishers need to see from authors. I know when a message or story is clear or captivating, and I know why it's a foolish idea to write a book that is "for everyone." I also know what it takes to get your book out into the world and I can tell you this: it's not for the faint of heart.

So, in this season, after meeting many faint hearts, I came up with a solution of something I could do to try and help...I decided to share everything I knew about publishing! I wanted to pull back the curtain and demystify all those things authors have to figure out themselves by going down Google rabbit trails or straight-up guessing. Does the chicken or the proposal come first? How do I know what a publisher wants in a proposal if I can't get an agent? And how do I get an agent if I don't have a proposal?

There are many unknowns.

The solution was to put everything *I knew* down on paper and invite strangers into a group video messaging app called Marco Polo so they could ask me every question they've ever wanted to ask a literary agent. In March 2021, I led my first cohort of five authors through a month-long intensive of telling them exactly what I tell the authors I represent to do for a proposal, like how to clarify their content and audience, and put together a relational marketing plan, among other things.

I call it "relational marketing" because most authors love the writing but hate getting the word out about their writing. And whether writers like it or not, you can't write a book, print off a bunch of books at Kinkos, and put them in your basement and hope people will knock on your door to ask if you've written a book that they can purchase. The romantic idea of a secluded author anonymously sending off their manuscripts to a publisher only to be met with rave reviews and a first print run of a million copies isn't really happening anymore. Maybe Banksy could do it, but for most of us, we have to do some leg work.

Sure, many writers love being in solitude *as* they write, but the process of getting what you wrote into the hands of others is a whole different story. Traditional publishing or self-publishing, it doesn't matter. You have to call on your connections and relationships to help you get the word out, and no one understands the necessary aspect of this more than other authors.

Every known author had a season where they were unknown.

Some weren't even known until after they died.

Not really the direction we were hoping you would take this foreword, Joy.

I always find putting things in perspective of life and death actually reframes a lot for us humans, so I always weave in a little fatalism wherever I can.

Back to what I was saying…

Not everyone wants to write a book in their lifetime, and a very small percentage of the people that say "I've thought about writing a book" will actually ever do anything about it. But people like Leslee, Jodi, and Rachael, the creators of The Unknown Authors Club, and all the authors you will read in the subsequent pages *are* doing something. Many have become friends, are cheering each other on, and have a bond of doing something together to pull out and refine the craft that is deep within each of their souls.

It can be discouraging for those soul writers to see celebrities and people with large platforms getting book deals not necessarily because of their love of writing, but because a publisher could safely calculate a decent number of sales. Unfortunately, the world of publishing rarely feels fair.

My observation is that the hardest part of being an unknown author these days is the struggle between doing what everyone is telling you that you need to do to get your writing published, and also making sure you stay true to your voice and the pure love of the craft. That's why in hindsight, I realize that the best by-product of the cohorts I started wasn't necessarily the finished book proposal everyone gets, but rather the friendships that are formed to keep fanning the writing flame.

The Unknown Authors Club is 100% the embodiment of that by-product and has reached beyond what I could have imagined. The friendship and camaraderie of Leslee, Jodi, and Rachael has now created a space for writers who feel alone and unknown in this process. They are creating the season before the season.

And the unknown season, to me, is the one filled with the most possibility and purity.

— Joy Eggerichs Reed
Author of *Get to the Publishing Punchline*
Paris, France

xiii

Book Deals and Brilliant Personalities
by Leslee Stewart

Growing up in Oklahoma, my next-door neighbor, Harold, never called me by my name. He and his wife, Carolyn, had lived next door long before our house was ever built. By the time my young parents moved into our house, Harold and Carolyn had reached retirement age with their children grown and moved away.

It didn't take long for family lines to blur and for Harold and Carolyn to become an extra set of grandparents to my sister and me. We had an open-door policy between us, and I took full advantage of it. Almost daily, I would bound across their front lawn and walk right into their house, without so much as a knock. Their kitchen table overlooked the front yard, and Harold, who was usually seated reading the newspaper, would see me coming and holler at Carolyn, "Hey! The 'Liddl'n's' coming over!" For readers who don't speak Okie, "Liddl'n" was Harold's way of saying, "Little one." With Harold, a nickname wasn't so much a way to tease you as it was a term of endearment. If he called you by a nickname, it meant you had a special place in his heart, and I happened to be the only person in my family he called by any name other than my own.

As I got older, "Liddl'n" went by the wayside and was replaced with a new nickname, "Personality." I'm sure this second nickname had a lot to do with the fact that I had a penchant for the dramatic. Whether I was telling a story or tattling on my sister, I did everything with a good amount of flair.

As the story goes, Harold started calling me "Personality" after seeing a TV commercial promoting a local business college, a place where people could learn specific, in-demand office skills like data entry, typing, or dictation. In this commercial, a bubbly, young lady arrives at an office to interview for a job. Dressed in a pale pink suit, she sits down across the desk from someone who the viewer assumes must be the hiring manager. The camera is aimed directly at the young lady and only the hiring manager's hands are visible in the foreground.

The hiring manager's voice opens the commercial.

"So, you're ready to start a new career," he says to her. "Do you have any business training?"

"Well, not exactly," she responds, quickly plastering a big smile across her face, "But I have a brilliant personality!"

"What about dictation skills? Do you know how to do dictation?" the manager asks next.

"Um, no, but I have a brilliant personality!" she responds, this time waving her hands to emphasize just how brilliant her personality really is.

"What about computer skills?" he reluctantly asks next.

"No, but I have…" and before she can respond with her standard line, the hiring manager interrupts her, "I know, I know. You have a brilliant personality!"

The video freezes and another voice comes over the commercial, "In today's business world, personality alone won't get you very far. Let our business college train you for your next career today!"

While I'm sure Harold's decision to call me "Personality" was made out of love mixed with a tad of jest, I understood his (and the commercial's) message: my brilliant personality alone wasn't going to be enough in the future. I needed to learn a skill and work hard to be considered somebody in this world.

So that's what I did. I knew I wanted to write for a living, so I went off to college to pursue my dream of becoming a journalist. I excelled in school, landed a dream internship at a newspaper, and even spent a few years as a reporter after college. My hard work and sharp writing skills soon opened the door to corporate America where I spent nearly two decades leading communications for a few *Fortune 100* companies. I was doing exactly what that commercial had taught me: using my training, skills, and work ethic to climb the corporate ladder. So, when I eventually left corporate America to become an author and write my own stories, I never imagined my exceptional writing skills would be the last thing a publisher would want from me.

The truth is, if a publisher made that same commercial today in order to sign a new author, the remake would go something like this:

Publishing Exec: "So, do you have any social media presence?"

Me: "Not much. But I am a brilliant writer."

Publishing Exec: "What about going viral? Have you had any TikToks go viral?"

Me: "Uh no. But I am a brilliant writer."

Publishing Exec: "How many subscribers do you have on your YouTube channel?"

Me: "I don't have a YouTube channel, but I am…"

Publishing Exec: "Yeah, I know, I know. You're a brilliant writer."

In today's publishing world, signing an author with a brilliant person-ality—a.k.a. someone who's known, followed, gone viral, and been retweeted—seems to be of higher value to a publisher than their ability to write a great story. Many first-time authors get book deals based on popularity, not because they have something particularly profound or interesting to say to the world.

As somebody who doesn't normally shy away from the spotlight, I'm not afraid to put myself out there when it comes to promoting my writing. But the expectation for a new author to already be somebody—to be followed by tens of thousands of people before a publisher will take a chance on them—was something I hadn't bargained for when working on my first book. The truth is, being unknown is the curse of great storytellers in the social media age.

Authors have traditionally been reclusive, introverted, and painfully awkward when it comes to media or self-promotion. Popularity is the last thing they think about and it's never the motivator for writing. They just want to pen great stories and leave the promotion up to the publisher. Sure they'll be happy to do an in-store book signing, a reading, or give a media appearance here and there; still, traditionally, authors have not been entirely responsible for the majority of promotion when it comes to putting a new book into the world.

But those days are gone. Today's author needs to not only be able to pour their heart and soul onto the page, but once they're done, they need to be able to win over an audience with a relatable, likable, interesting, extroverted personality. And to keep that audience coming back for more, they need a highly visible, frequently-updated social media presence, which usually shows them wearing a fedora, giant glasses, and drinking a nitro cold brew with oat milk from a sustainably-sourced, locally-owned coffee shop. I've got the giant glasses (thanks to middle-age vision), but am pretty sure I'm past the fedora-wearing stage (thanks to middle age). Oh, and I prefer my coffee *old school*, (made in a normal coffee pot at home, served with a splash of store-bought creamer).

As an unknown author who dreams of being published, this leaves me at a crossroads. Do I choose the expressway—spend time and money trying to go viral and quickly grow my followers in hopes of a publisher deigning to say yes and offer me a contract to publish my book? Or, do I choose the back roads—self-publish my book, grow my social media organically, experience the highs and lows of being unknown, but stay true to myself throughout the journey?

Regardless of which road I take, the final destination is the same: I want to be published. But in today's world, it might just take a brilliant personality to get there.

All in Good Time
by Karen deBlieck

Writing began as a hobby. Something I squeezed in between changing diapers and cleaning the house. A secret thing I did after I tucked the little ones into bed. I dreamed of publishing a book but only in the way that children dream of unicorns and dragons—far away and (most likely) imaginary. Back then, I didn't mind being unknown. I was still finding my way around the writer's world. Gaining writing friends, attending conferences, and learning how a novel went together.

But soon, when I became more serious about publishing a novel, I realized I had to step out of the shadows and share my most vulnerable thoughts and feelings with the world. At the insistence of the professionals, I began a blog and made a profile on Facebook. I gained followers but not anything too exciting. Enough to show the rest of the world that I existed. There wasn't a lot of time, however, to fit blog posts, social media, and writing a novel into my day between homeschooling and tutoring.

I've learned patience on my journey as I've felt so close to publishing a novel for so long. People enjoyed my poetry and short stories. Numerous people have read my works and encouraged me on my path to publication.

With my first novel (a Young Adult fantasy) I nearly obtained an agent. The agent had shown interest in the project, and we emailed back and forth. We planned to meet at a large conference and have further discussions. But when a critique partner won an award, the agent signed her immediately. Of course,

I was excited for my friend, but it was a hard pill to swallow. A few weeks later, I emailed the agent and they'd already filled their one speculative fiction spot with, you guessed it, my friend. This devastated me, but I shook it off and continued on.

I shopped that project for a long time but, like many first manuscripts, I discovered it contained major flaws that I didn't have the skill to fix. Looking back, I can see that it was my "practice novel." So, I set it aside. (Don't worry! I still think about the day that I'll pick it back up again.) At that point, I noticed there were a lot of speculative fiction writers and not that many spots in the industry, so I began to work on something completely different.

My next novel, a historical retelling of the biblical story of Samson, took a while to write as I was also working for a not-for-profit (that supports Christian writers in Canada) that didn't have a lot of boundaries regarding work hours. For three years I had very little creative energy to write. But when I finished it the end result pleased me—the best writing I could produce at that point in my writing journey. I invited feedback from other writers and friends and received a positive response. Readers were excited and eager to see this book on the shelves, affirming the story's importance. Music to my ears! So I sent it out into the world. I queried many agents to try and find it a home, but everyone found it too dark. They were looking for positive stories that dealt with race.

In 2018, I won a scholarship to attend a conference in California. There I met up with two editors from larger publishing companies who wanted to see more. Once home, I submitted my manuscript, and both responded positively with an invitation to resubmit after increasing the word count. Once finished, they began the process of considering it more seriously. This was a huge breakthrough, and one I wasn't expecting!

This same year while attending a different conference, I met the woman who would become my first agent. I'd sent my piece to her agency before, but she confessed she often rejected submissions based on the title. (The title of my book was *Sam*…does it help that the tagline was "some lines aren't meant to be crossed?" No?) While at the conference, I decided to approach her after she taught her class. A few weeks later, I was her client. She was a big New York agent, and I'd done my research on her (as far as I was able), preparing a litany of questions and looking into the deals she had made in the past. She hit the ground running, checking in with the two publishers already considering Sam and choosing a few more to query. I was ecstatic, and I started a new project.

At first, communication was good. She checked in with me several times to get details and let me know she was circulating Sam to publishers. But soon, there were great delays between emails. Sometimes, I would contact her and get no response.

Being a new writer, I wasn't sure how to handle this, and I hated to bug her, but I continued to get in touch. Then the pandemic hit, and I decided I needed to give even more grace since everything was so chaotic. Soon, our communication slowed down to a crawl with no new submissions (despite promises of a second round) and no updates on what we should do moving forward. After reaching out one more time in 2021 with no response (and some nudging from my husband and writing buddies), I terminated our partnership. We met virtually for a close-out meeting, and she seemed genuinely surprised that I wanted to leave.

She could very well be a fantastic agent, just not the right one for me. Her communication with me wasn't great and she focused a lot on the selling side without giving me much guidance as a new author. I realized, through this partnership, that I was looking for someone who would support all of me as an author not only my current project. Not that they had to babysit me but, if I had questions about social media or which story ideas had merit they'd be willing to touch base.

It was only when we parted ways that I discovered all the submission info, along with the manuscript and my proposal, had been buried with her old intern's stuff. The intern had left a year and a half earlier, which meant my novel had been sitting there all that time, forgotten.

When I spoke to an agent friend, I found out this can happen with some agents if your books fail to sell quickly, especially if you're a quieter client. Any agent hates to always bring bad news. So new authors, don't ever feel guilty about touching base with your agent. Contacting them monthly is acceptable.

By this time, my leads from the two big publishers had dried up. Both had been heading to the editorial board, but I never heard back from either as to the status or even the why. This was a hard blow. I'd been so close to getting my book published and not only had it not been accepted, I had no idea why, or if there was any way to fix it or my craft moving forward. This was both my highest high and my lowest low.

Once I dug myself out of the valley of "woe is me," I doubled down on my most recent project, which is also the one I'm pitching now. It's garnered a lot of interest in pitch events on Twitter and caught the interest of some editors at the Society of Children's Book Writers and Illustrators conference. I was still hesitant to start a new agent partnership since my last one had gone so poorly (and I wondered if anyone would want me?). I'd learned the hard way that no agent is better than a bad agent!

While trying to figure out querying both my old book and my new book I reached out to an agent who was representing my friend to ask a few questions. He asked to have a Zoom meeting to discuss and during that meeting, he offered to represent me in the new year. Funny enough, we'd met before when I was working for that not-for-profit. Back then he'd been an editor with a large publisher, and I'd been doing my job helping other writers. Now he's my agent and I couldn't be happier! He not only believes in the works I've done but also in my dreams for the future. That's a big thing! And I'll admit, he's talked me down from the imposter syndrome ledge once or twice. I may still be unknown but having those who encourage you on the path makes it better.

Besides, being unknown has its perks. When you forget a link to your blog post on social media or make a cringe-worthy mistake, there's no crowd pointing it out. The goals and deadlines you make for yourself are yours and yours alone. No one's waiting with bated breath for your next masterpiece. Plus, you're still a surprise. The best is yet to come! You can explore different styles and genres without worrying about losing a big following. Enjoy the freedom!

Obviously, there are downsides to being unknown as well. Watching writer peers who "started at the same time as you" holding their brand-new book babies in their hands. Reading a published story that's not that great but so close to your book idea. Rejection after rejection after rejection. Feeling like no one likes your stories (or you). Not having any fans who adore your characters as much as you do. It can be hard to be unknown.

I've been working on my writing for ten years and probably the last five years with a laser focus. It's tough out there and a pandemic and supply chain issues haven't helped! The most important thing that's kept me writing into the wee hours of the morning is the belief that everything happens at the right time. I wasn't ready for publication all those years ago. I don't think I would have had the strength or the fortitude to weather the scrutiny.

Ten years ago, I desired to make my mark on the world, especially after surviving breast cancer. A fear that my time would run out sooner than later drove me. My desire now is to share hope and my love of stories with others. My identity and value are no longer wrapped up in what I write. Ten years ago, I was homeschooling my four children, three of whom have special needs. Now they're thriving young adults which frees up more brain space for my creative endeavors.

Besides, I've grown as a writer. What was my very best work at the beginning of my journey is much different from my best work now. I'm capable of tackling those bigger subjects and themes that once intimidated me.

I'm also thankful I had the time to find myself as a writer. Some writers are instant successes, but that forces them to find their footing in the public eye. I've enjoyed the quiet of working with my group of writing friends. And I'm certain I'll enjoy celebrating with those same friends when my first book gets published.

As to what keeps me going—before, I would struggle with the "what ifs" until they paralyzed me. I'm not going to lie, they still plague me occasionally, but I'm able to remind myself why I'm writing and that I'm being obedient in using my God-given gifts. And that's all I must do. Produce my best work. And not get tangled up in the rest.

Taking my eyes off the prize of publication and fame has made me a better writer and brought me a great deal of joy. Joy in the process itself and learning new things.

Still, I look forward to the day that I'm recognized, receiving fan mail that includes pictures of my reader's favorite characters, or letters sharing how my stories changed them. Until that day, I'll be in front of my screen, butt in a chair, writing my heart out on the page.

The Best Kept Secret
by Blakni Riley

Disclaimer. Food is my jam. If I believed in reincarnation, I would swear that I was a chef in my past life. I love it that much. When I travel, I am routinely hunting for places to eat. Sometimes it doesn't work out, but most of the time I leave as one seriously happy patron. As a matter of fact, there is this scrumptious Mexican food restaurant in my hometown that serves food nothing short of magical. It is practically life-changing, outside of choosing Jesus. It is *that* good. Staunchly authentic to the culture, you leave nourished in ways more than by your belly.

Fun fact. This place does zero advertising for their restaurant. No billboards, no social media blasts, no requests to "like and subscribe." There is no meticulous pouring over of the data, no fretting over algorithms to generate more traffic. No one loses sleep over a follower count or whether or not they will finally get a name drop from someone who is already recognized as "somebody." Nope. Their focus and gumption are tailored towards honing their craft day in and day out in order to turn out a product so satisfying, that customers begin planning their next visit before they even payout from their current one.

Visit with any writer and *this* is where our hearts are. We want to provide such a space that our readers want to keep coming back for more and bring a new friend along for the experience as well. We strive to craft stories and put words to experiences that leave our readers affected in such a way that they are forever changed. We work to bring light to everyday life.

Everything else that comes with a desire to write for the masses is often the very thing that halts writers at their keyboards, sometimes permanently. Why? The push to create, develop, maintain and tirelessly pursue a "platform" for the promotion of our writing is nothing short of daunting. If we aren't careful, we get sucked under the tidal wave of validation, or lack thereof, and become frozen or feel like the words we've been given to pen are cheapened by the blue check of verification. When I even speak the word "platform" I feel like I should do so through a whisper and my hand over my mouth like I'm uttering a piece of profanity and I'm scared my momma is going to catch me.

I just want to write. There are pieces that begin forming from the crumbs of life experience that marry with language the Lord provides me, and it becomes an almost insatiable urge to produce a product simply to allow the thoughts to subside. Like a well-seasoned dish, time and spices blend to create something delectable. That is where my heart resides.

I avoid all "dis" that can come with a focus only on the business side of writing. Discontent, disconnect, disbelief, discouragement: like a wise person once said, "Ain't nobody got time for all 'dis." Or "dat," but you get what I am saying. This is the worst environment for an author to sit in because it becomes the catalyst for a ceasing of the gift we've been given as writers, which is the communication to tell the stories and share the lessons. The number of times I have personally stopped and started because I was more worried about whether or not people would read what I wrote, rather than actually worrying about the hearts that would read it, is really embarrassing to share. I believe transparency, however, is the only way to get to a place of real work, so here we are.

As a self-proclaimed word nerd, I derive a certain enjoyment from looking up words and their various definitions. Did you know that platform does *not* mean a social following? In every format that I read, platform means a place to operate *from*, not on, unless used in the physical sense. With that information, it is safe to say that every single person who writes from a rooted position, does indeed have a platform. That is where their heart beats best. It just appears hidden because they stand on it instead of operating from underneath it.

This is actually what propels me to keep writing when the pressures around me dare me to stay silent. Much like teenagers who say "you won't" as fuel to ignite a challenge, I say, "challenge accepted." The words that pour out of me and onto pages allow me to process life on this side of heaven and give a boost to dig in when circumstances want to scream louder. They allow me to see the gift of the seemingly ordinary and connect it to the extraordinary. Even if I am the only person who ever realizes the connection, then so be it. When they have the opportunity to reach more than me, that is part of the beautiful bonus. My job is to plant and water. Where the blooms emerge is less up to me, and more up to my God who has granted me the very breath I breathe. Rather than begrudging the hidden seasons I've walked through, I'm learning to appreciate them.

Sheltered seasons are absolutely necessary for the authenticity of the writing process. It is there that humility takes precedence, and our vulnerability goes unchecked. In the hidden space, there is the cultivation of a masterpiece. Much like a painting by Michelangelo or Van Gogh, time and space must be allowed in order for all bets to be off. Otherwise, we run the risk of placing value on the frivolous and wasting the one commodity we truly never get a return on, which is time. We have to allow for the curing, and resist rushing the process for the sake of being considered "known."

The fact of the matter is, we are already known. We have been since before we were formed in our mother's womb. Psalm 139:17-18 reminds us that our Father's thoughts about us are precious and cannot even be numbered. We can't even count them because they "outnumber the grains of sand!" There is no greater knowing.

Maybe that is the best story for me to express as an author. That is, after all, the platform from which I write.

In a time where a distorted version of the term "platform" has become the golden goose by which success is measured, gifted writers remain hidden from a world that desperately needs the strength of their testimonies. I heard recently that moments are created in thirty-second increments, and that those moments become memories that are repeated and relayed from one person to the next for the rest of the person's life. Our words are that powerful. They have the ability to change the trajectory of generations to come, long after we are gone.

As pieces take shape and stories are sculpted, they simply need an avenue to release them to the hearts intended to receive them. Never reserved for the elite only, each one stands ready to touch the soul of everyone who comes in contact with it. The power of connection is the ultimate reward.

Perhaps the time has come that we move from our hiding places and allow ourselves to be truly seen. What if the way we use our gifts is exactly what someone needs in order to recognize that they too are known and meant to be seen?

Much like the restaurant in my community that is creating from their roots, authors are the same. Dreaming. Building. Crafting. Fine-tuning. Enjoyed by those who know, and available for those who have yet to meet them. Not for the sake of being seen, but for the ability to break bread and share what they've been given to bless others.

Satisfaction guaranteed.

Author Unknown
by Don Pape

There is an ancient saying that goes, "Home is where the heart is." Well, today we left home.

The call came I guess around 4 a.m. I was still deep in sleep.

Then my mother poked her head into my room and quietly whispered in my ear to wake up.

"It's time to go."

That was all she said.

That was all I needed to hear.

Where we were headed was unknown. But we knew we had to leave.

My mother's work as a translator was no longer required. Her heart was broken. There were no more options for her and life as we knew it was to disappear by the end of the week. Plenty of office workers had already packed and left. Stories filtered back that several of her colleagues had caught earlier flights and were settling into a newfound life of freedom.

Last night at supper she had gone over all the preparations necessary for leaving. For heading to the airport. For a hoped-for departure to somewhere that was not war-torn. Not so chaotic. Safe.

She made sure I had packed the right clothes. She was concerned I would forget something or, worse, put something in the small travel suitcase that was unnecessary. She kept reminding me that traveling light was the key.

She stuck her face in one more time making sure I had gotten out of bed.

I had.

I was now in a light t-shirt—remember, travel light is our motto—and a pair of jeans. They were my favorite pair.

She looked down at my feet and shook her head.

I had put on my leather sandals. My favorite. We had them made for me a summer or two ago. Before the pandemic. Before our lives had changed. Before when we could go to the markets and shops without wearing face coverings. I mean "masks."

My mother's face said it all. She was not happy with my footwear.

She was not in the mood for frivolity. Her face was drawn and a somber mood enveloped our apartment. Her unknown status with the Embassy jeopardized her life and our future. How could people turn their back on somebody who had served them faithfully for so long? My mom was proud of her ten-year service pin. I saw her removing a framed picture that identified her with the foreign power now leaving. The certificate attached to the back was quickly shredded into small pieces.

I looked up to the top shelf in my cupboard and reached for the shoe box.

When it arrived from my grandmother it had been very heavy.

It had taken almost two months to reach us here.

In the toes of each shoe had been a can of soup. Delicious and tasty that mother had used as gravy at the holidays. The rest of the box had candies, wrapped in cellophane, scattered throughout, stuck in every corner, and surrounding the shoes. The wrapping called them "Jolly Ranchers."

Mother opened a drawer, finding some socks, while I pulled the box down and prepared to put the sensible shoes on, ensuring the shoelaces were tied before I was reprimanded again.

***

We walked into the waiting area.

What normally would have taken us twenty minutes from our apartment had now turned into a very long and complicated drive. Our neighbor drove us. He would take a turn and go down half a block and then suddenly veer right or veer left, coming down the Russia Road and in a back way. It felt like we were inside a video game. The speeding up, slowing down, turn left, turn right was upsetting my stomach and I was grateful I had yet to eat something.

Even at this early hour, crowds were everywhere.

Soldiers—both good and bad—stood guard and appeared menacing, without uttering a sound.

Fathers carried luggage—even bundled and tied coats—while mothers pushed strollers with babies. Many of the little ones, unsure of where they were headed, screamed as if to say, "Get me out of here!" My mother knew where we had landed, had spied an opening into a back entrance, and had found us a quick entry into the busiest part of the terminal.

And now we sat and waited. I thought of another saying from my grandfather, "Hurry up and wait."

I watched the pudgy little boy toddle in front of me. He was exploring a whole new world and, unlike the rest of us, was enjoying all the commotion. His mother eyed him nervously, keeping somewhat of a distance while repeating, "Don't go too far."

I rolled my eyes. How far could he go?

My mom cooed at the little guy and asked his mother, "What's his name?"

Again, I rolled my eyes. What did it matter? The airport terminal was crawling with people, all of us with status unknown, with everyone's lives at risk and status undetermined.

***

I watched the boy out of the corner of my eye.

While he was likely middle grade, he was making every effort to shirk his childlikeness and behave maturely in front of my little one. He pretended like he had no use for the "baby" but I could see a smile forming on his face. Whilst he feigned disinterest his mother was quite lovely, asking after his age and name. I recognized her from a few all-staff meetings at the embassy. When we both realized we were scheduled on the same flight we also recognized that her corps of translators had been just down the hall from my colleagues in communications and media. My position had not been classified since I was a press liaison and I hadn't been in the office very long before I had gone on maternity leave. I was lucky to have had that position since I had been grandfathered in quite likely because of my husband's role at the nearby base.

Now, here we all were, sandwiched into a stifling departure lounge, one overhead fan trying to cool the heads of over one hundred people in a room that would best accommodate sixty. Back home the fire marshal would have a fit. I wasn't even sure they posted room maximums here. Another influx of people—families with strollers and suitcases, soldiers bearing arms—pushed people along, shuffling Veeda against her will away from her son. I thought of her name and with my minimal knowledge of the language remembered her name meant "found." And here we were, a sea of humanity, ever crowding, ever frightened. Ever lost? Where were we all headed? Would flights still get off the ground? Rumors were already spreading. I knew family awaited us in Ohio, but I could not imagine the future for this dear woman—my sister—and her sweet son.

It was hard to believe that only 24 hours earlier I had filed my last report, an update on the chaotic two-week withdrawal process, to Reuters. Hitting "send" on my borrowed laptop, I dated it, leaving the byline *Author Unknown*.

Why I Write

by Cindy Arnold

"Why do you write?" she asked as she opened our coaching session on publishing. I stared back at the Zoom screen, sifting through the layers of my answer.

How could I explain that I've been a writer for as long as I can remember? That writing was my first hobby and my most passionate pastime? That writing is both how I teach and how I learn? That writing is what my heart yearns to do even when my mind cannot find the right words?

How could I concisely tell this professional I'd just met why I write when it's always been a part of who I am? I thought of Scout describing reading in *To Kill a Mockingbird*; I cannot remember learning to write for others—it's simply always been there.

"Well," I stumbled. "I think I want to write to share with other people what I've learned."

"Great!" she masked a wince, and I guessed my answer was likely generic. Common. Unimpressive. "What have you learned that you think your audience would like to learn, too?"

"That it's okay to not know much at all," I chuckled.

We kept talking and refining my author's purpose, her coaching questions helping me unearth more specifics than I had originally expected.

But after the session, the question stuck with me for days.

Why do I continue to write?

At one point, not long ago, I had stopped writing. Had given it up altogether. But even then, I was startled by a similar question.

"So why aren't you writing now?" he had asked.

"I do miss words." I had shrugged despite knowing it wasn't a video call. I'd just told him about the papers I had written in college, the ones I submitted to the conferences for presenting, the ones I submitted for scholarships, the ones I'd written and rewritten for hours alongside my mentors. The ones that had helped with student loans and that extra semester of classes. He'd only known me in my current number-driven role, not one that connected me to words.

So why aren't you writing now?

I listed off responsibilities that kept me too busy to write, ones that neither of us believed were as all-consuming as I implied, and we moved on with the conversation. But words looking for an audience kept whispering in my mind.

Words are always in my mind. Always. I can think of only one moment in my entire 37 years when my mind did not have words in it, and it was fleeting and monumental. Spiritual. Even sixteen years later, I am still amazed at how simultaneously my mind could feel full and yet empty of words.

Weeks passed after that phone call. I talked with two different friends about their blogs and the importance of drafting, and then I brought drafting up again with a student lamenting about timed writing assessments. I picked up journaling again, started a list of what I was grateful for each day, and considered a second trip through a 100-day social media posting challenge, each time searching for a way to record my words. I had so many of them, but I didn't know how to share them or where to send them. Who would want to read them? Why did I want to share them?

I wrote more poetry than usual, thinking people might be willing to read about my mundane experiences as long as they were in verse. Oh, and if they were paired with a picture—it seemed it must have a picture—then people would surely read it. I typed up my travel journal from my last trip overseas, a vulnerable one for myself and an abridged version that I shared with the rest of my travel team. I wrote a sermon on that adventure, and I collaborated with a friend on another sermon, too.

And then more words pushed to the front of the crowd, demanding an audience. I stood in my kitchen, fork in one hand and bowl of scrambled eggs in the other, holding two separate verbal thought processes simultaneously:

> *Every time I make Mom's noodles, I start off thinking*
> *I've forgotten how to do this. It'll come back as*
> *soon as my hands start moving.*

This will have to be a longer poem than usual.
I have to say the part about the muscle memory
taking over—kicking in—no, taking over.
This poem will make T. S. Elliot look concise.

> *Use my hands to mix the eggs and flour,*
> *add more flour to the sticky ball in the bowl,*
> *move this slightly less sticky*
> *and much larger ball*
> *to the rolling pad, and—*

Now it smells like Grandma's house.
That will have to be a line all its own.

What if I just make this one prose?
There's too much they need to know
that would just be left out of a poem.

The flour is flying everywhere—
it's on my shirt just above my waist,
just like Grandma's all those years ago...
Mom was wise to insist on
a shorter counter in her kitchen.

Some people read essays.
I think they publish books of them.
Blogs are probably taking the place of essays.
But who would read this?
It's just me making noodles.

So why aren't you writing now?

His question echoed again.

I knew why I'd left words for a while. Because when the words were painful, or confusing, or lonely, or frustrating, or even just unsure, I didn't want to leave evidence of it. For heaven's sake, what if my grandkids found it someday? What an awful legacy...

...a legacy of truth. Of learning. Of growth. Of reflection. Of grit. Of the journey.

My fist immediately found the pressure the noodle cutter needed, but I frowned at how the noodles stuck in it. I shook my head. I sprinkled in more flour and, like the women before me, I blamed the humidity. I sifted the noodles between my fingers, breaking them apart, and letting them fall back into the bowl where the ball of dough had started. Again I picked them up, sprinkled them into the boiling broth, mine from an aluminum can instead of the re-purposed plastic butter bowls I'd grown up knowing.

Maybe I just don't know the audience yet.

So why do I continue to write?

Connections.

Some days, I write to connect my own ideas, to connect the dots in my life that are otherwise floating around haphazardly. I write to connect the abstract to the tangible, the physical to the spiritual, the simple to the complex. But that's why I write for myself, not why I write with an audience in mind or hope for publishing.

And yet, even when I share it and work toward this grand goal of publishing, I still write to make connections—connections between me and my readers. I want someone to read my unique, irreplicable experience and feel connected, to know our similarities within our differences. (Not in spite of them, you see. The prepositions matter.)

Just like when I remind my math students that I also make mistakes, I want to tell my readers that we don't have to aim for perfection or have it all together, and we certainly don't have to learn it all on our own. I want to tell them I am with them in the confusion and the clarity alike, the highs and the lows, the faith and the doubt, the growth and the plateaus, and even in the regressions. I want to tell them they are not alone, and I want to believe it for myself, too.

I write to connect, and publishing will create so many more connections than I can foster on my little Instagram platform. I write to connect with you, too, dear reader. As long as I'm an unknown author, I hold hope for all the connections that have yet to form, all the ones yet to come.

Being an Unknown So-and-So
by Jodi Cowles

Her face was huge. Giant. Massive. I don't know if you're quite getting the picture—her bright, unnaturally-white teeth took up an entire window, her faultless coiffure was sprayed to such inconceivable heights it had to wrap over onto the roof, and her brilliantly-blue eyes that perfectly coordinated with the well-chosen suit were as big as my head.

This well-known author whose name I will not tarnish by mentioning, arrived at the very gates of the National Booksellers Convention in a 45-foot Class-A motorhome with her image plastered across the side. Larger. Than. Life.

As she alighted, there may or may not have been a cloud of rock star fog pulsing around her before she was quickly surrounded by a phalanx of payrolled-personnel ushering her through an admiring crowd that parted like the Red Sea before her glittering presence. I'm not sure how long she graced the *hoi polloi* who sold her books with her exalted self, I had my own job to do.

You see I, in a difference minor enough to be negligible, arrived at the back door of the National Booksellers Convention in a beaten-up, Class-C RV named Bertha that I'd barely managed to nurse up the road as white smoke barreled out the backside from a busted transmission. I'd left Bertha in a distant parking lot with other members of the unwashed masses too broke to afford a conference-affiliated hotel. And even though I turned on the generator to run the air conditioner for an hour to pre-cool myself and my staff (cat) from the sauna masquerading as summer in Atlanta, by the time I'd hoofed it 20 minutes to the conference center while fighting my slightly off-kilter wheely bag full of books to hand out, I was drenched. My poorly-chosen t-shirt was wet, my Supercuts-hair stuck haphazardly to my forehead, and I don't think anyone even held the door for me, let alone paved the way with rose petals, asked for my autograph, or invited me on a national press junket.

That, my friends, was one of the many differences between being a known and an unknown author twenty years ago—the entrances.

Another minor difference was the fact that this well-known author probably had 500 people working every minute of the day to transform her words into bestsellers, movies, and even scented candles full of kitschy inspirational sayings. I, on the other hand, managed to get ten minutes of undivided attention from my hybrid publisher and watched in a sort of out-of-body-amazement as she glad-handed me through the room like that scene in Jerry Maguire.

At that moment I tasted what it could be like to be known. And then, *poof!* It was over almost before it began. I schlepped my broken wheelie bag back to my beater RV where I found my staff (cat) so overheated I laid a bag of frozen corn on top of her and she actually stayed still for ten minutes trying not to perish.

Fast-forward twenty years. That known author is still churning out a book or two a year, and her staff has no doubt swelled with the need to manage the mini-series, the scented candle and knick-knack empire, and the ongoing tempest of promoting someone who was once a lowly you-and-me but is now a *brand*.

And me? Well, I don't like to brag, but about six months ago I somehow managed to catch the attention of a random bot farm in Eastern Europe and my Instagram following swelled to over 2,000 (mostly fake, mostly Middle Eastern) followers. I finally gave up on blocking them because, a) it took too much energy, and b) I enjoy making fun of their creative and typo-licious efforts to spam me.

Since that summer at the convention, I've written a couple more books and sold a few hundred of them, including several copies to people I don't even know! In other words, in terms of my writing "career," twenty years of effort later, I am still unknown.

However, in real life, I've had a glimpse of what it's like to be known in the small, village-like community neighborhood in which my family and I live in Istanbul, Turkey.

It works a little something like this. We get picked up in a taxi in another part of town by a driver we've never seen before and he says, "Oh yeah, I know you. You're the Americans who live up the street from me and you rent your place for X amount of money from my cousin's cousin's ex-husband, and do you think you could teach English to my nephew and get my aunt a visa to America?"

We've been watched, analyzed, and gossiped about for almost eight years. I've wondered if it's a little like being a celebrity, except in place of paparazzi I have *teyzes* (Turkish for auntie) in their wild, any-pattern-goes outfits watching my every move from their second-story windows and reporting it to the neighborhood gossip network.

In place of people writing nasty comments online, I have everyone and my literal neighbor telling me to my face that my daughter's not wearing enough layers if she doesn't look like the Stay-Puft marshmallow man during winter. And there's no such thing as quickly and anonymously sneaking up to the store in pajamas to buy a roll of toilet paper. I've been caught and had to say hello too many times. But at least there's no one snapping photos!

It seems all I had to do to be famous was move halfway around the world, and I'm not sure I'm a fan. But thankfully, my "fame" is geographically limited and quite specific. Just call me a micro-celebrity. All I have to do is leave my neighborhood or this country for that matter, and I'm back to being a good old, unknown so-and-so.

But even as an unknown so-and-so, I still have a dream. It may be preposterous to hope to see my words in lights, but I keep going all these years later when even my staff (cat) has long since retired. Why? For the pleasure of pure creation and the joy of giving life to the words that are always trying to bubble up out of me.

Getting a publishing deal or celebrity book club endorsement seems a little bit like winning the lottery, but following a calling is something different. In that way, I know I have something in common not only with that celebrity rock star author, but with every other unknown author slaving away in their basement at 3 in the morning, or the coffee shop over their lunch break, or for the ten minutes they have while waiting in the pickup line at their kids' school.

All of us authors in our own way are trying to connect, to be known, and sometimes we'll even sweat blood in our effort to reach through our words to touch people's hearts.

And yes, most of us are and will continue to be unknown to most of the rest of the world, but even that's okay. Because the words have to come out and in getting them down we find joy. Finding an audience on top of that is fabulous. It's the dream, but it's not the joy.

I hope in reading these few words of mine, I've become a little less unknown to you. And if you want to read more of my words, just know that there's an author out there with a similar name writing bodice-rippers. So for heaven's sake, on that Amazon search, be sure to spell my name right!

Recognized But Unknown
by Maren Heiberg

As I walk the switchbacks up and down this mountain town, sometimes I stop in my tracks. The environment around me, the place that I have known for almost fifteen years, all of a sudden feels unfamiliar. I know where I am, but I get this sense that it is so foreign to me. Although I walk the same streets every day in this pedestrian town, things just all of a sudden feel so strange. It is like a movie and it only happens for a split second. But things get silent and everything inside me says, "How did I end up here?" Fifteen years and it still happens. I all of a sudden feel so out of place and everything feels so different than everything I have ever known. I shake it off, chalk it up to me still learning about this place and I move on with my day. Maybe my mind needs to remind me not to get too comfortable.

Fifteen years ago, I moved to this South Asian town in the foothills of the Himalayas. There was nothing familiar, nothing known to me about this place. I came to work with a non-profit and ended up staying far beyond my commitment. It is a love story, not as romantic as the movies, but a love story nonetheless. I met my husband here only a month into my stay. We were friends first. A few years later we started dating and then, got married. We keep choosing each other ever since. Through the years, we have built a family, a life, and a community.

After fifteen years in this small town, you would think that at least some people would know me. I am one of only a handful of white "foreigners" living in this city in the foothills of the Himalayas, our sweet little town of 200,000 people. It sounds like a lot, but for South Asia, this is a small town. It functions as a small town. I cannot walk down the street without being noticed. People whisper about me as I walk by, but the English word "foreigner" always can be heard. The people in my neighborhood all know who I am. Despite living in four different apartments in fifteen years, they have all been in the same neighborhood. I stand out like a sore thumb. It is hard to not be recognized in my town. Sometimes I can overhear people talking about me and they think they know my story. They whisper to their friends something they believe about me. Maybe they do not know that, although I am not fluent in the language, I still can understand a lot of what is being said. The stories always have a bit of truth in them, but they are never fully accurate. Sometimes I am European, sometimes I am American, and sometimes I am just a "foreigner."

The descriptions of how I got here or what I am doing vary from story to story. Often I am stopped on the road and asked about my three boys or how my father-in-law is doing. I quickly realize that they are talking about one of the other white, foreign women that live here. I am American and I do work with the community in a non-profit, I have a son and a daughter, my father-in-law passed long before I ever met my husband, and I am a writer. Sometimes, however, you just go along with it, because it is easier to play along than to explain that you are not the person that they think that you are. You kindly smile and nod your head, and then you text the other foreigner about the interaction and laugh together.

Working in community development, I spend a lot of time getting to know other people. We ask a lot of questions and even visit a lot of houses. You get to know a lot about people in the community. One of the greatest victories for me was when I heard our local taxi driver tell another driver that I was a local. It meant so much and I felt seen. Not known, but seen. After 15 years, I have learned a lot about the culture. However, the majority of the community actually does not know me. They think they know me, but really they have no idea. There is a huge difference between being recognized and being known. There are a lot of assumptions. Preconceptions of the Western world and the things that people have learned in movies have prevailed. I spend a lot of time asking people personal questions, but there is not a lot of reciprocation, and that is okay. It is even expected. I came here to serve the community, so I do more of the question asking.

In 2020, just as in every place worldwide, we were hit with the pandemic. COVID entered the scene with an explosion and I became even more recognized and even less known if that is even possible. Fear of travelers had people who did not know me wondering if I had come from a foreign country recently and brought COVID with me.

Amid the chaos and the unknown, I decided to tackle a dream. A dream that started several years before to write a children's book for this South Asian town. I desperately wanted my kids and other kids to understand the beauty of the place where they live. That it is unique and deserves to be celebrated. However, with the authoring of the book, I realized how unknown I can be, even to the community I have built here. My in-laws and extended family here have never asked me about my life or my family. Even some of my friends do not know much about me. Many of them do not know that I am a writer.

When I launched the book at a local café, several friends, colleagues, and educators came to the party. I have spoken to leaders in the community about the book and it is selling in a café in the heart of the town. The book is all over social media. However, I remain the "foreigner" married to the Nepali man, who frequently walks with her kids through the town square.

Being recognized but unknown can be lonely. It can be disheartening, but with those who have taken the time to know me, those are special relationships. Being known is not important to me. However, I want people to know my book, *The Adventures of Pandi the Red Panda*. I want it to not only be recognized but to be a part of people's childhoods. I want them to grasp the celebration of this community, the place I have highlighted in this book, and in the books I would love to write in the future.

The Opus of My Life
by Rose Booth

One of my favorite life-affirming movies is *Mr. Holland's Opus*. It's the story of Glen Holland, a musician and composer, who takes a teaching job to pay the bills while he works on a symphony—an opus—that would make him rich and famous. His world becomes busy and chaotic as he and his wife have a beautiful boy who is deaf. Along with his personal life stresses, Mr. Holland spends time outside of class helping to grow and mentor each student who shows a need for additional help.

As the movie comes to a close—*spoiler alert*—funding for music in schools is cut and Mr. Holland is forced to retire. In the last scene of the movie, Mr. Holland's wife meets him at school as he is cleaning up his room and leads him down to the auditorium. There, assembled on the stage, is an orchestra full of his former students. One particular student, Gertrude, who he mentored on the clarinet, is now a state senator and delivers a speech on behalf of all his students. Her tear-inducing speech ends with, "We are your symphony, Mr. Holland. We are the melodies and the notes of your opus. We are the music of your life." Gertrude sits back down and they offer Mr. Holland a baton to conduct this orchestra in finally performing his opus.

I never watch this movie and don't sob at that ending. A simple man has spent his entire life caring for his family, shepherding his students, and putting his dreams on the back burner. Then when his time teaching music was done, he was rewarded with the opportunity to conduct an orchestra consisting of the fruits of his labor, playing the one symphonic piece he'd spent a lifetime writing. Man, it gets me right in the feels.

I've longed for many years to become a writer. I was a feature editor on my high school newspaper staff and scored an interview with the county superintendent for my first article. I have worked in technology publishing for more than thirty years and wrote a blog for twelve years. But my "opus" was a book. Oh, how I wanted to write a book.

In 2005, I decided to start a blog. During that time, blogs were on the rise and I was hungry for something to get my creative juices flowing. I had been in a job for a year prior that zapped every bit of creativity out of my soul. I worked for an insurance agent. Even the sound of the job makes you yawn. It was a good job, but a trained monkey could have done it and there was no gray, only black and white. In fact, my boss said to me once, "Rose, you need to dumb down to do this job." That was a sign I needed to get out. Not long after that statement, I was approached about coming on board a new startup technology company that was being started by folks I'd worked with before. I was elated! Almost correlating with my first day on the job, I started my blog, *Ruminations and Reflections*.

I kept that blog going for twelve years before I let it go, but during that time, everyone said, "You should write a book!" The ideas were endless. First, I would write a devotional. Yeah, that's what I'll do! Many of my blog posts were like devotionals, so I thought I could easily compile them into a book format. Working full-time I just didn't feel like I had the extra time or the knowledge of where to even start. Let's be real, it was intimidating so I didn't pursue it any further.

Then it changed to a book on being single. I even got as far as an outline for that one. I'm a never-married gal, so I thought I had some good insight on being single. I was in my forties at the time and had longed to be married. I was an old soul who was less, "I am woman, hear me roar" and more, "I am woman, get my door." In my twenties, I just expected marriage to plop right in my lap, and when I hit twenty-eight, I thought, "Hmm, did I miss something?" Then when I crossed over the forty mark, I figured maybe this life of singleness wasn't so bad. I sat down and wrote an outline for "Party of One." Of course, life got in the way of that "opus." I began serving in the college ministry at my church. I spent most of my time outside of work meeting with college girls who were struggling. My shock factor was eliminated as I heard almost everything imaginable from these young souls. My heart and passion was to help them steer the cars of their lives and I didn't have time to write a book on being single. I was living it in front of them.

From there my opus changed to a book on mentoring and discipleship for the local church. I was discipling many young women both in college and in careers and began co-directing my church's women's ministry. My passion for discipleship was growing and not many churches were doing it effectively. Of course, I thought a book on that topic would be magnificent. I was able to speak to women's ministry leaders and churches and felt like I had a good framework for a book. But, I realized I didn't know how to start. I reached out to a friend in Christian publishing and got no response. I decided to put it on the back burner, as maybe that was a sign it wasn't the right time. I was busy discipling young women most nights of the week after work so I didn't have a lot of extra time for my "opus."

In later years, I contemplated a book on leadership and management. During my day job, I managed a team that represented sales support and junior salespeople. The part of the job I loved was the people management; which most people hate. I felt like I had a unique way to meld the management of professionals and managing their whole person which was something the business world needed to hear. But life got in the way. I worked full-time, taught Bible studies at my church, and continued to mentor many young women over the years. My "opus" went on the back burner yet again.

In November 2019, my life took a drastic turn. I became septic and almost left this world. That event would start a two-and-a-half-year health journey that led to fourteen surgeries, two heart caths, and almost a year in hospitals and rehabs. In that span of time, I found myself facing death two more times. It culminated in December 2021 with the loss of my right leg above my knee. Though I was devastated, I pushed forward and am still recovering back to life. I realized when life took a turn, it opened a door for me to truly write a book; an autobiography of my loss and my miracles.

During this span of two and a half years, I heard about a writing cohort where I could spend an intense month cranking out a book proposal. I was so intrigued. This was finally an opportunity to put my "opus" to paper. I applied for the upcoming cohort, which was taking place in March 2021. Due to a setback and patella tendon tear after knee replacement surgery, I had to back out. I was devastated. I had a book in me ready to go! The literary agent who led these cohorts assured me of a spot in the future.

I spent the spring and summer of 2021 trying to heal from the patella tendon tear. Another cohort was happening in October 2021. I contacted the literary agent and asked if I could join and I did. I got all the prep information the week before it would start and discovered my knee was infected; so back to the hospital I went. At the last minute, I had to back out and my "opus" dreams were delayed once again.

The next five months were brutal in the hospital and rehab, but I made it home in March 2022. There was a cohort happening in May 2022. Do I dare even consider it? But I did. I reached out to the literary agent again and asked if there was a spot. She said yes and I began to pray for protection so I could participate in this cohort. My life had taken so many twists and turns I didn't have much faith that the third time was truly going to be a charm.

When May 2022 came, I was physically well and ready to tackle this cohort. On the other side of those four weeks, I came out with a 42-page book proposal, tears in my eyes, and a renewed energy to write again. As I work on expanding my network, pitching my book, and writing with fervor again, this unknown author's passion has been reborn. My "opus" is formulating and if I never become the next best-selling author, I know God will use my words to inspire others to carry on in their passions.

My favorite Disney princess is Cinderella. When I received my book proposal, I felt like I'd just got invited to the ball. If, or more positively, when I receive a book deal, I'll feel like that glass slipper slid right on my foot with no problems. Our dreams, and our opus, always have a chance of coming true.

Calling Myself a Writer
by Bethany McMillon

The morning summer sun creeps across my porch as I sit, feet up on the coffee table, reclining and contemplative. In minutes, I will be within the sun's already sweltering reach. Sweat droplets slide down the side of my glass of iced coffee. I swallow the last of the sweet, creamy, vanilla concoction and chomp down on a piece of the now coffee-flavored ice. My thoughts swirl, searching the depths of my brain, struggling to remember the story ideas that danced through my mind in the middle of the night. The connections between a memory, a Bible story, and an encouraging word made sense at 2:00 am, but now that my laptop is open and my fingers are paused on the keys, the ideas flit in and out just out of my conscious reach. I wonder, in dramatic fashion, if my time as a writer is over. Have all my ideas been exhausted?

Ernest Hemingway reportedly said, "In order to write about life, you must live it." Closing my laptop as the sun's heat reaches my toes, I mumble to no one, "I'm not sure sorting laundry counts as living life." But sorting, washing, drying, and folding are all must-do items this morning.

Inside, I rinse my glass and set it in the sink. Feeling thankful for the air conditioning, I move to our closet and pull the laundry basket into the bathroom to sort the colors—darks, lights, delicates, and the occasional red or bright blue. The dark piles grow quickly as I toss shirts and shorts and socks. I pull the towels off their hooks and create a new pile for them, too.

As I carry the first load the few steps into the laundry room, I consider all the words I've mentally sorted after they've been written—some too personal to share, some humorous or fun, and some meaningful and connection-rich. Perhaps it isn't that words have dried up, but instead the too-personal words of my recent journals are like our pile of dark clothes—ever-growing. The words meant to share are rarer, like the reds. And I haven't been wearing (writing) many of those lately.

I shove the clothes into the washing machine and try to remember the first time I knew I wanted to be a writer. There's evidence of an early desire in the boxes of mementos on the top of a closet at my parents' house—a story about a duck, named Ducky, carefully scribed on primary lined paper. There's a vivid memory of third grade me turning in a self-assigned paper, entitled "an S.A. about Friendship" to my teacher. I giggle to myself as I pour detergent into the dispenser about the idea's root—an episode of *Little House on the Prairie*—and the substitution of "S.A." for the actual word essay. Grown-up me still cringes at the memories of red marks across the pages of my junior English papers and exhales with the memories of encouragement within my senior English class. Written words have always been plentiful—passed notes in junior high classes, journals I (literally) burned as a young adult, and typed out memories I didn't want to forget.

I push the button to start the wash cycle. It dings and whirs, ready to work; then I hear the water rush into the bin. Memories of moments that ticked me ever closer to the idea of truly calling myself a writer flood my mind.

***

I clutch the steering wheel of my parked car. The gray light of the just setting sun casts shadows across my seat and I consider pulling away before the writer's meet-up even begins. No one knows me; it's my first time coming. They won't know if I just go home. They are all probably *real* writers with published books and a million accolades, not just-a-blog-site-only-her-parents-and-a-handful-of-friends-read writer. I steel myself as I pull open the car door and walk toward the restaurant, attempting to switch my mindset to that of a writer ready to learn instead of a beginner ready to quit and return to her personal journaling only. I pull open the restaurant door, warm light and the wafting smell of bread greet me as I glance around for a group who looks like they might be writers. Seeing only one group with laptops and pens, I plaster on a smile, introduce myself and join them. During our meeting, we share project highlights and discuss questions or hardships within our craft. As I listen and hesitantly participate, a thought runs on repeat: At what point will I feel like a real writer?

***

Just before the workday begins, I tap the email icon on my phone to give it a quick scroll. My heart leaps into my throat. I jump from my chair and stand as I read the message. "They will be delighted to publish my piece," I whisper to the empty room. I'd posted weekly on my personal blog for months, but my first acceptance from other writers and editors felt like the approval of an exclusive club…Will this publication experience add validity to me calling myself a writer?

***

"I printed your blog this week and gave it to a woman who works with me," he mentions just before our church life group begins this Sunday morning. My thoughts fly back to the moment just after I posted the words I'd written that week. I'd wondered, briefly and vulnerably, if anyone was reading or considering any of the thoughts and stories I posted. He tells me about the young woman and why he thought she might benefit from the article. We chat about how long I've been writing and what my plans might be for future publication. As class begins, I pause still stuck thinking: *He reads my blog?* I

47

am a writer whose words are read.

***

I rip the tape off the box and squeal. The books are here! I gingerly lift the first copy out of the box and thumb through it. With its rose gold cover and crisp, clean pages, full of carefully chosen and vulnerably written words, it is a warm hug of friendship and camaraderie. For months, I'd worked with a thoughtful and diverse group of moms to bring this book to fruition. The title, *Strong, Brave & Beautiful: Stories of Hope for Moms in the Weeds*, describes our hopes for the stories in the book—hope for other moms. The words I'd written, examined, and edited, now here in actual print. I stage a picture or two and post them on my Instagram page. I then open the back door and plop down on the couch. I find my name attributed to one of the short stories and my eyes well with tears: I am a writer whose words are on the printed page.

***

I blink, pulling myself back to the laundry task at hand. As I open the dryer and unfurl the first of the towels from this load to fold, an idea floats to the surface of my mind. This time, instead of thinking I'll remember it the next time I sit down to write, I set the towel on top of the dryer and hurry to my laptop. This time, my fingers fly across the keyboard. It is the pull to share the stories floating in my head and the desire of my heart to encourage others that draws me to my craft again and again; the words DO come, if only I give them space to speak. Slowly I'm learning—I am a writer.

The Tennessee Transplant
by JJ Barrows

After eight years of living in Southern California, my husband and I up and moved to the more affordable land of Chattanooga, Tennessee. There was minimal adjusting for me, having been born and raised in the South, but I thought surely my husband would have a harder time. Josh is originally from Alaska, which might as well be worlds away; I was shocked when I first learned Alaska was a part of America that was attached to Canada! My mountain man husband was about to be in shock, or so I thought. But as it turns out, Alaska has a lot in common with the South... pride, guns, and "get off my land." They're basically country folk without the accent. Mind you, not *all* Alaskans. Josh is humble and doesn't own a gun or land, and so it is with southern living—we aren't *all* rednecks, but there's a large population of them in the South (and a little redneck in all of us).

Other than churches and Walmarts overtaking Starbucks for every street corner in the South, the biggest difference from West Coast living has been yoga. Joining a yoga class in southern Tennessee looks a lot different from Southern California. For starters, *bread*. It's often the topic of conversation in my Tennessee class, everyone salivating while in side plank. Apparently, there's a bakery in town called "The Bread Basket" that not only serves up amazing bread, but decadent pastries. Our teacher listed out each one she had tried over the weekend; the cheesecake brownie was not her favorite, but it was in front of her so she ate it anyway.

"My husband does that," a middle-aged woman called out as we switched from right side plank to left, "I don't get it, how can you eat something you hate?"

"Hate is a strong word," Joe, a middle-aged man transplanted from Chicago, yelled out from the other side of the room, "No one said they hated it, just that it wasn't the best… but I agree, if it was just sitting there in front of me, I'd eat it too." Most of the class agreed, and the teacher stood her ground as well, not just in her side plank but in the cheesecake brownie, "If it's just sitting there looking at you, you can't *not* eat it."

"So JJ," Joe says, addressing me since I'm the newest person to the studio, "you'll start to notice the only thing we talk about here is food." I laughed, "Oh, I did notice," I said, "and I love it. In California, all they eat is tree bark!" The whole class laughed, and I remember thinking the sound of that laugh felt better than most of the stretches I'd just done.

"You're right!" Joe yelled as he pointed at me, "Out there on the West Coast, I went a few years ago, beautiful resort, all they served us was twigs and berries, I was like 'Where's all the food? You call this a buffet?'" I laughed at Joe's very obvious Chicago accent that he says "has gotten better" since living in the South. "The best class of all is next," Joe says as he rolls up his mat, "my favorite class… lunch!"

The ladies all agreed, one mentioning she was trying to avoid Taco Bell and may have to swing by Zaxby's instead. "See ya later, California," Joe said to me as we walked to our cars. "See ya, Chicago!"

When class ended, I thought about how funny it was to be doing yoga while intermittently talking about bread and cheesecake brownies the entire time. *That would never happen in a California yoga class*, I thought to myself, and I laughed as I mimicked the conversation the whole drive home.

I love that my Tennessee yoga class is an older group of people who are trying to take care of their bodies but can't quite bring themselves to give up bread. As Joe says, "It's a classic!" I hid the fact that I was gluten-free so as not to elicit any groans or typical questions like "what's a gluten anyway?" I do enjoy finding really good gluten-free bread, but it's just never going to sound as good as the more simply put "bread." Joe's right, it's a classic.

To be honest, I thought my transition from California to Tennessee would be a lot harder. I miss the ocean and still feel it tugging at my heart from time to time, but knowing I have planned visits keeps me sane this far inland. Outside of that (no ocean), I really love it here. It's simpler and more laid back. The people are kind and not trying to compete with each other. The pressure I always felt to do more, be more, make more has gotten quieter. It's not that I don't feel it at all, but I feel it much less, and certainly not on a daily basis.

This past weekend, I was able to perform in a comedy club for the first time since COVID cleared my calendar two years ago. Turns out standup comedians were deemed non-essential during a worldwide pandemic. Who knew? Laughing, however, is *very essential*, so comedians burned themselves out trying to make people laugh virtually. As a comedian who feeds off audience reactions, it was awful. I was excited to get to perform in my new town, but also nervous because even though I now call Chattanooga "my town," I'm still the new kid on the block. Deep down, I didn't feel the right to call it my town yet, but I also had the desire deep down for the neighbors to welcome me in and affirm I'm home.

I worked Thursday, Friday, and Saturday writing, editing, crafting, and reciting my ten-minute set. Three days of work, all for ten minutes.

I wasn't sure how I was going to be received by the crowd, no "unknown" comedian ever really is. That's currently what I'm called in the entertainment industry, "unknown," whether for writing, comedy, or art, it's always the same response to any submission I turn in, "Being an unknown, we can't risk not having a guaranteed audience." My favorite was from a publisher who said, "Your writing is strong and stories are relatable, but being an unknown, I'm not sure who would care to read your work."

Yea. That one stung a little.

So, in order to become known, you can't be an unknown? Did we all not start somewhere? I hear older comedians or even musicians complain about how easy kids have it these days to make it big. "We didn't have social media," they say, "we had to do *real work* out on the road." Though social media has given comedians and musicians an easier platform, it's also given *everyone* an easier platform, making the market so saturated that the standard to be noticed is a minimum of 300,000 followers (and that's for an "unknown").

With people scrolling and swiping through content so fast, it's less about talent and more about statistics—most of those stats being your social media following and what you can already bring to the table aside from your talent.

But! I was given a shot this past weekend. Without having a huge following in this particular area, The Comedy Catch in downtown Chattanooga took a chance on me. Okay, they actually had me audition, but it was in front of a live audience in the hopes of getting booked as a feature or headliner in the future. That was good enough for me and the only chance I needed.

I'm not sure how to describe it other than I felt like I had finally found my people. The crowd was electric! And as I navigated through my transition to Tennessee, growing up Southern Baptist, and surviving middle school, it seemed the audience had been through it all as they keeled over in laughter; almost making me forget what I was going to say next because I was caught so off guard by the volume of their laughter. The show went so well that the club asked me to stay and perform for the late show which I was not originally scheduled for.

While that sounds like a dream, I almost said no because I had not mentally processed performing twice in one night. I get anxious easily and I was feeling so good after the first show that the thought of performing *again* made me nervous… *again*. Plus, what if I didn't do as well? I wanted to end on a high note.

It's funny how I can complain about not being given a shot and then as soon as I get one, I realize how late it is and how much more comfortable my bed sounds. Josh encouraged me to stay for the second show, "I really think you'd kill it twice," he said. I nervously agreed, and he was right—I realize "unknowns" probably aren't supposed to say this, but I killed… twice.

I was flying high on adrenaline Saturday night and well into Sunday evening. But so it goes with entertainment that by Monday I was starting back over, submitting footage to clubs, asking to get booked, only to be met with the same term, "unknown." The higher you ride on the adrenaline, the harder the fall when you come crashing back down to reality. Even now I feel like a total basket case, the paranoid kind that Green Day sang about in the 90s: "Do you have the time to listen to me whine, about nothing and everything all at once?" My mind playing tricks on me… *I killed, right?*

I had to remind myself that just because I worked up the nerve to perform two back-to-back sets (and killed both of them), it didn't mean that every club in America needed to line up to book me, though sometimes it feels like they should. I pulled out my journal this morning and noticed a quote I had written in it last year by Brené Brown, *"Don't shrink back. Don't puff up. Stand your sacred ground."*

"Yep," I said out loud, responding as if Brené had just said it to me, "I didn't shrink back this weekend, I showed up… but then I think I puffed up." Which is why I was feeling so discouraged—it was the puff deflating, reminding me I still have work to do. "Now to live in the tension of the two," I said, "neither shrinking nor puffing." I took a deep breath and laid down on the sacred ground that is my bed, "I just gotta keep plugging away."

I checked my email and received two more rejections. "Don't shrink back," I whispered.

And now, on with my day...

The Unknown Me
by Samantha Stewart

H ave you ever looked in the mirror and not recognized the face staring back at you? Or have you ever looked through the pictures in your camera roll and thought, *who is that?* I know I have. That's because the person I see when I look in the mirror today is very different than the person I used to be.

My transformation began in May 2021. I took my husband, who was sick and needed treatment, to the hospital, and then, because of quarantine regulations, I had to leave. But before I left him, we agreed that we were standing in faith for his healing and, at the same time, we were going to partner with the power of science to get him healthy and back home.

Despite the battle going on around us, I had this unexplainable peace that my husband would return home completely healed. My faith never wavered when I got another report from the doctors or when I gave consent for yet another procedure they believed might help. During this battle, when I would look in the mirror or look at a picture of myself, I did not recognize the woman staring back at me. I had never seen her before and did not really know she existed. The woman I saw looked tired and yet alert, concerned and yet hopeful. She was being strong for her husband and daughter, and yet cried herself to sleep often because she felt weak and ill-prepared for the battle she was facing. In the midst of it all, she began to journal her feelings, concerns, prayers and the events of each day, even though she'd never really written before. This was how she/I started writing.

Seven weeks later sitting in a cold, ICU room, surrounded by family, we said goodbye to my high school sweetheart, my husband of almost 24 years, my boo. He was kind, he loved God, and he loved how creative our Creator is. His smile could light up a room and there was just something special about that twinkle in his piercing blue eyes. For 28 years I had identified as Jason's girl, so now what? Who was I without him? Losing a spouse is scary, but what is just downright terrifying is not knowing who you are without the person who has been by your side for so long. I had become the unknown me. A wife grieving the loss of her husband. A widow.

After Jason died I kept writing. I began pouring my grief journey onto the pages of my journal thinking maybe one day it would help someone, even if that someone was me. Initially my writing began as a way to journal all that we were experiencing in the early days of being in quarantine, being in the hospital, and later as he was sedated in the ICU. After he passed away, I kept journaling because it was a way for me to express all that I was feeling, thinking, and walking through while beginning to process all of the grief.

The next thing the new, unknown me did was take all that private, journal writing and start a blog. Even as I was hitting publish on making my private journal public, I was not completely sold on the idea. I have never considered myself a writer until this experience. Growing up, I was the Sporty Spice of my class. I would rather challenge the boys to a game of 1-vs-1 on the basketball court than sit with my feelings and write. Throughout school, I was never told I was good at writing and I was never confident in myself enough to put pen to paper (yes, I am that old).

Grief is such a solitary adventure. Grief is solitary because each person grieves differently and there is no one right way to grieve. Grief is solitary because there is no end to grief, but by processing and sharing you find that you are able to grow around your loss and pain. Writing out my story, week by week, has revealed God's hand of faithfulness and provision in every step since losing Jason. The written pieces of my story reveal my family and community support has been monumental in my healing. The act of writing my story has allowed me to be comfortable sharing my story face-to-face with people I meet. In doing this we inevitably find common ground in grief, even if our losses are different. In sharing my story I have found that people who were once so awkward in talking to me or just flat avoided me have begun to engage in conversations. They have started to ask me questions about how to talk to people who are grieving. This is why I believe that more people should be open in sharing about their own grief journey. This is why I am writing and sharing my journey!

I gave up the title of wife for the title of widow and became the unknown me. In an effort to find me again, I wrote. I wrote first as an outlet for my emotions, and yet I found that the more I wrote, the more I felt empowered and responsible for sharing my story. Even though I did not recognize the woman in the mirror, I never felt abandoned, forgotten, or alone. The peace that was with me when Jason was in the hospital, is the same peace that is with me in my grief. I was surprised to find that writing out my feelings and emotions was easy. Being vulnerable, posting to the blog, and allowing others into my journey was difficult.

I often wonder who outside my close circle finds and reads what I write. I often wonder if they are walking through great loss as well and if so, do my words bring comfort or pain? I write because I am getting to know this unknown me. But, I mainly write because by being unknown and obedient to share, my Heavenly Father becomes known and is seen and shared throughout my story. He is weaving a new piece to the tapestry of my life and I love sharing the journey!

Today, as I look in the mirror, the woman standing before me is stronger than I ever thought possible. More than that, in the heat of the battle she stepped toward her Heavenly Father instead of away. She didn't get bitter and blame God. She didn't get depressed and sulk over every bad thing, and everything that did not go the way she had planned and/or prayed for. Instead, she chose life, she chose love, she chose Him. She chose to believe that her Heavenly Father was good even when life wasn't. She chose to believe that God was faithful when she was lacking faith. She is resilient. She is a fighter. She is me. Soon the unknown me will become more fully known, but until then I will continue to write, share, and declare the good works that my Heavenly Father is doing in and through me.

Stay tuned. The adventure is just beginning.

In the Wilderness
by Dani Nichols

I hear the wind before I feel it—it starts rolling off the mountainside with a whoosh and a whirl, then I hear the groaning and snapping of branches and the aching of deep-rooted trees. Finally, I feel it—it pulls the hair from under my ball cap and whips it into my eyes, it brings color to my cheeks and acts like a disrespectful toddler, tugging on my nose. I see puffs of dust climbing up around me, and the waving of tall trees in their dance with the storm, in their ancient wisdom they bend, and so do not break.

The wilderness is almost never quiet, it is not peaceful. We want it to be, we talk about it that way. But always the forest is creaking and whooshing and settling and groaning and wiggling with life. It just isn't the sounds we associate with noise; there are no blaring car horns or boomboxes or sudden shouts here. But a few hours in the woods and you'll think you hear the voice of someone just out there. *Did I hear my name?* You might think to yourself. You'll see a shadow and wonder if it's a mountain lion or a bear. More often than not it's just a menacing tree stump.

My horse, Buzz, regularly sees predators where there are none. I jokingly call him the "Yeti-hunter" because while we're riding through the wilderness, he's quite convinced of mythical baddies around every corner. However, the biggest danger in the wilderness is ourselves. Buzz might jump to the side only to snap a tendon, or knock me off onto a rock. We are at risk from our own lack of foresight—hunger and thirst are much more likely to kill the backwoods traveler than a mountain lion.

But oh how we fear the unknown of the wilderness. We fear gleaming incisors and silent footfalls and stealthy predation much more than we do our own mistakes, even though the latter is much more real and deadly.

I'm in the wilderness now and reminding myself that a granola bar and a water bottle are greater survival tools than a .44 magnum. An even better tool is the will to walk. I am not the best horsewoman by far; I am easily frightened and easily knocked off course. But the one thing I do have is a bountiful supply of perseverance. One foot in front of the other, I tell Buzz, and he snorts but does so, thinking that this crazy human of his isn't nearly concerned enough about the perils of being something's lunch.

I'm thinking about the perils and beauties of a wilderness ride as I am also in a creative wilderness. It's easy to see writing as a war-like act, the way my horse sees a trail through the woods. It's easy to think that someone in publishing is calling out my name with malicious intent, that my rejections are indeed personal, that those sagebrushes and undergrowth are shaking with predatory energy.

A few years ago, I wrote a memoir I was really proud of. To my amazement, it was a finalist in a prestigious writers' conference contest. I got a babysitter, kissed my husband, booked a hotel room, and drove to the conference, just to see what I could do with my little dream. It felt like the closest I'd ever come—I'd won a few small contests and gotten some publication opportunities, but this was a chance to be recognized for a real book deal. I had a proposal, a one-sheet, and a list of contacts. I was shortlisted for the grand prize at the conference. This was my chance to leave the vagabond's life behind, I thought, to get off the trail and onto a paved road for once.

But within hours of arriving at the event, I realized that a dream and a quality manuscript is not enough—the wilderness is cavernous and insatiable, it creeps in even when we try to lock the windows and bar it out. Every agent, publisher, and editor had the same sad smile, the same questions about why

I'd been on the trail so long, why was I so alone, and why was no one following me on my trek?

They smiled at me when I asserted my desire to write like one picks a trail through the woods, like Dani Shapiro and Anne Lamott, Joan Didion and Brian Doyle. They were kind but not hopeful—there was no way forward for me to create books like the ones I admired, at least not without a bigger following. I looked at myself in the mirror of the hotel room and watched my eyes fill with exhausted and disappointed tears, one moment I felt rage, and the next despair.

It's tempting to pack heat instead of lunch. It's tempting to make the industry into the bad guy, to snarl at Amazon and our e-obsession, to bemoan everyone else's lack of taste. At a meeting with a particularly kind editor, she told me how impressed she was with my writing. "This is a moving and powerful story, and you've written it beautifully," she said sincerely. "Would you consider rewriting it into a devotional?"

The message was clear. She could sell a devotional but not a memoir, she could help me achieve a partial dream of publication but not the whole thing. There was a stop for my wilderness journey just ahead, but it wasn't the resting place I had dreamed of in my years of wandering. As much as I wanted to say yes, to gain reprieve from the rattling winds and startling underbrush of the wilderness, I knew that God had given me a different calling than the one en vogue at the conference.

I didn't win the competition that weekend. I said no to changing the tone and style of my book. I opted for more wandering, rather than a bed that didn't feel like mine. I came home frustrated and felt like a failure, so I tacked up my horse to let out my feelings.

The wind comes rushing down the mountain, bending trees and playing with my hair. Birds explode from the underbrush and Buzz startles, quivering beneath me. Am I sure that I want to be here, in this land of insecurity?

I pat his neck and tell him, "Easy boy." He nickers at me and stomps his forefoot, fear gone as the wind has whirled by us. The simple answer is that yes, the wilderness, for all of its danger and unease, is home. It is the place my soul loves. My dark mahogany saddle rests comfortably in the curves of Buzz's back and I know what he's thinking, I know when he'll be afraid, and I'm ready to comfort him. My eyes awaken to the beauty of the northwestern high desert. I love the brilliance of blue jays in deep-green pines, the dusty gray-blue of the mountain sages, the deep rust-red of a hawk's tail as he circles above, riding the wind that just caressed my face. I love the rugged outcroppings of black basalt, crusted with hundreds of years of lichen, and the craggy junipers standing guard above them.

The wilderness is exhausting and unforgiving, it requires know-how and courage to exist here. But more than anything else, the wilderness, both on horseback and in writing, requires perseverance. Writers write, the old saying goes, and while I imagine it's easier to write while in a parade surrounded by adoring fans and the sounds of success, perhaps that's its own mythology, like the imaginary predators we see behind every rock. Much more likely is that every form of creative expression is its own wilderness, that one foot in front of the other is actually the only way forward. Just as predators are not nearly as dangerous or numerous as we imagine, neither is the reward of the dream publishing deal or a rocket ship to success as satisfying and fulfilling as we hope it will be.

So I saddle up in faith, doing the thing I love, the thing I know how to do, telling the truth as I see it. I ride because I can, because it brings my body and mind into alignment, because it gives me joy even though I know I will feel afraid, inadequate, and even hunted. I write for the same reasons, because the wilderness is home, because beauty is worth bringing attention to, because the trail is long and the days are short, and somewhere, someday, out in these woods, I will hear my name.

Keeping My Fingers on "F" and "J"
by Tanya Motorin

I f I'm being completely honest (and I'd like to be), my relationship with the unknown can be a little conflicted. The unknown feels exciting when my husband surprises me by getting a sitter and spontaneously takes me to a new date night spot. This kind of unknown brings my curiosity to new heights and I start feeling giddy just imagining the trendy decor, tasty dishes, and enjoying a relaxed conversation where we get to finish our sentences without being interrupted by one of our three (adorable) children. Did I mention they are adorable? This is the unknown that provides much-needed space to breathe and connect with my favorite human. If all unknowns were this wonderful, I'd be the first in line for a new "choose your own daily unknown adventure." However, as we've all experienced, the unknown can also bring about fear, anxiety, and that dreaded loss of control.

On my 46th birthday, I answered a call from the doctor that I'd been anxiously awaiting. When the phone rang I locked eyes with my husband, and motioned for him to join me in the bedroom as I put the phone on speaker and closed the door behind us. We held our breath as we waited for what felt like days before hearing the words, "Invasive Ductal Carcinoma." It sounded like a foreign language, but I knew what it meant. Breast cancer. After I hung up I stared at my husband as my eyes filled with tears. He reached out and held me close as I silently wept. *How was this happening?* I wondered. In an instant, I sensed fear and uncertainty rising inside me as I was handed the most devastating unknown I had ever faced. Once my new reality began to set in, more unknowns weren't far behind. *How would I get through this? How could God allow this? Where would I get my treatment? How would I find my doctors in the midst of settling into a new city? Where would we live? Was I going to be okay? How would I navigate these new waters as an unknown patient without my trusted doctors?*

Nearly four years have passed since this devastating diagnosis shook my foundation. In the midst of the aftershocks that followed, I felt God impressing on my heart to write about my experience. I wasn't sure how I would do that since I had never written a book, and most days I barely had the energy to get my kids off to school so that I could crawl back into bed or head to yet another doctor's appointment. Regardless, I couldn't let go of the notion that I needed to get my experience down on paper. I felt burdened. Responsible. Compelled. Like there was a force within me driving me to get my words on paper.

It started with some ideas that were bouncing around in my head like a ball being flung through a pinball machine. Maybe it was because I was sleep deprived from "sleeping" in a recliner for three months. As I fought the darkness in the room and filling my heart, there was no escaping them. One by one, these ideas were birthed into existence as potential chapters and I couldn't get them out of my head until I found a place for them to belong. I wished that my ideas would go away so I could sleep, feel sorry for myself, or just check out. But they persisted.

If I was really going to write a book, I would have preferred the topic be about something light and encouraging. Maybe a children's book about some hilarious thing that my kids had said or done, like when I walked into our adjoining hotel room to find my two-year-old daughter (who shall remain nameless) holding her poop in her hand. Or perhaps it could be a guide to having a beautifully decorated home, without having to spend your kids' college savings. Better yet, it would have been a blast to taste-test my way through Los Angeles in order to write a book about the hidden gems with good eats in the city of angels. Anything but a book about my journey with breast cancer.

Okay, so instead of me choosing my topic, my topic chose me. Now, in addition to being "assigned" a topic I didn't want to write about, having a relentless responsibility to get it out there, and zero bandwidth, I had no idea where to start or how one goes about writing a book. If all of that wasn't enough to keep me from moving forward, there were armies of doubts marching around in my head telling me that I had no business writing a book. After all, my high school Honors English teacher wasn't a huge fan of my writing, so who was I to think that I was a good enough writer to write an entire book? Not a booklet. Not a leaflet. A book. And who did I think I was to have the audacity to be a voice of courage, hope, and help for women facing breast cancer? *Wasn't there someone more equipped?*

My inner critic was my biggest hurdle, yet somehow, one day I picked up my phone, opened up the "notes" section, and began pulling one idea at a time out of the pinball machine and recording them as potential chapter ideas. Each time I opened up the note titled, "My book," I added more ideas until one day I knew it was time. Time to start writing. Immediately, another wave of doubt flooded over me and I was really starting to regret listening to God. *What kind of unknown path was He taking me down anyways? Who would ever want to listen to what I have to say...an unknown author with no credentials or books I could point to, to prove to everyone that I had earned a seat at the table?*

Miraculously, one day, I began writing. At first, the process felt awkward and uneasy, kind of like a middle schooler on the first day of school. I didn't want anyone to see that I didn't know what I was doing and I felt the need to prove myself. I wanted every sentence I wrote to be perfect the first time. I was hoping to be the prodigy writer who had no need for an editor (I was, after all, a teacher in my past life), but that process of trying to make it perfect the first time felt like a heavy burden and slowed me down worse than trying to run a marathon with my 1990s ankle weights. Once I gave myself permission to just get the words down, no matter how messy or not just right they were, I began to find my voice.

There were some days when the words flowed and I could hardly type fast enough to keep up with my thoughts, but other days were just painful. Painful not only because I couldn't say exactly what I wanted to say or how I wanted to say it, but because each time I sat down to write, I was stepping back into the most horrific season of my life. I had already lived it once, and now I was having to battle it over and over again. It was awful. I wasn't just up against your typical obstacles like writer's block and lack of confidence, I was also reliving the trauma I had barely just escaped. In some ways it was cathartic, but especially towards the end, it was actually prolonging my grieving process. I needed to be done.

As I inched closer to the finish line, it reminded me of how I felt when I was nearing the 36th week of my first pregnancy. Uncomfortable, irritable, and exhausted. Even though I was scared of all the unknowns coming my way, I just wanted that baby out of me. But there was still more forming and growing that needed to take place, so I waited for God to finish His job until it was time. Similarly, with my book, there was still more to be said, so I continued to show up (oftentimes against my will), and sat in front of the screen with my index fingers on "F" and "J" until there was finally nothing left to say. I had shared my story and had given every ounce of insight and encouragement I had to give. I was done! (Well, except for a tiny little part called editing). But each thought had found its way into the appropriate chapter. I felt both beat up and victorious! I wasn't sure exactly how I did it, but I had actually written a book!

The next morning I was all smiles until reality caught up to me and I realized that I was officially entering into the next season of unknown. Okay, so I wrote a book, but now what? I had no idea how to get published, or where to begin. Ugh. This whole process was starting to look an awful lot like life; just when you kind-of, sort-of figure out one season, you're onto the next and feel like that middle-schooler all over again.

I began asking questions and reaching out to anyone and everyone I knew who had ever gotten a book published. Again, I found myself learning a whole new language: traditional versus self-publishing, query, book proposal, literary agent, platform…blah, blah, blah. What I also quickly learned was that it didn't really matter how beautifully written my book was or how pressing the subject matter was, because no one (at least no one that could do anything about getting it published) was going to give a second glance to a book written by an unknown author without a platform.

I had no idea that being an unknown author would be the biggest obstacle keeping my book from helping the women I wrote it for. Like trying a new date night spot, I'm longing for an agent or a publisher to take a chance on me. To see my hidden potential, even though I don't have any Yelp reviews, yet. How do I get connected to that someone who lives for taking risks and uncovering a hidden gem? And how can I get someone who can make things happen to see past the fact that I don't already have a book published or have a following bigger than a small country? And where is that someone who will be the catalyst to bring help and hope that my words could be for the one-in-eight women diagnosed with breast cancer? I want these women to be known, seen, and practically cared for as they wade through the countless unknowns that come with a breast cancer diagnosis, but how can this happen if I remain unknown?

So, even though being an unknown author feels exhausting and defeating at times, and anxiety rises in me a bit every time my daughter asks me when my book is going to be published, I'm determined to finish what God set out for me to do. So, I will keep asking, seeking, and knocking until God makes a way. And all the while, I'll be keeping the one-in-eight women in my line of sight. Hold on ladies, help is on the way.

The Potluck
by Jace Schwartz

Sometimes, consuming the fantasy genre feels like eating yet another peanut M&M after you've already devoured half the bag.

On more than one occasion, I've gorged myself with peanut M&M's while watching the pilot episode of the next big fantasy show. That's when I think to myself 1) I've lost all self-control with my diet and 2) Does the world really need another dystopian coming-of-age fantasy drama? It needs another show about superheroes, or angsty love-sick magicians, or vampires, or whatever, about as much as I need another piece of chocolate.

"You're so right, Jace," I say to myself, popping another peanut M&M into my mouth.

Of course, this is all problematic because I love peanut M&M's. I'm also trying to write a children's fantasy series. And the real crux of the issue is this: if I were to take a stab at contributing to the exploding, voluminous library of fantasy out there, surely it would just be noise. Another piece of candy when we really don't need anymore.

I usually swim in these pitiful waters for a while, lamenting the elusiveness of originality. But originality aside, at this point I'd happily settle with the internal sense of simply knowing that I wasn't producing a carbon copy. With so much content out there, you can't help but feel like someone else beat ya to it! I cannot count the number of times I've watched something, or read something, and said, "Hey! That was my idea!"

I blame George Lucas.

The stars aligned, both in our galaxy and those far, far away, when George Lucas created his masterpiece that captured the imagination of, what feels like, literally everyone.

I was raised by parents who remember seeing *Star Wars* for the first time in the 1970s. They wax eloquent about the glory days when they paid four cents or something like that for a movie ticket (You know, back when they also bought their first home for a steep twelve thousand dollars). Those are my parents, and they were the same ones who passed on to us the gift of constant television.

My friends and I grew up on an obscene amount of television. We all watched the same stuff, all drew the Mickey Mouse ears at the bottom of the screen, all anticipated the next *Star Wars*, all got excited for the next *Harry Potter*, and all planned our Christmas breaks around the *Lord of the Rings* midnight premieres.

Do you remember midnight premieres? I do. And I am still not over their being torn from our cultural fabric.

I was a senior in high school when "Harry Potter 7.1" (that's what my generation calls the penultimate film) premiered, and I had graduated only weeks prior to the premiere of 7.2. I trust you see the implications here. I basically graduated from Hogwarts with Harry Potter's class.

And now, it's people my age, all Hogwarts graduates themselves—all with the same starry eyes, twinkling with the planets of George Lucas' far, far away galaxy—who are all working for Disney, or Amazon Prime, or writing books, all of them cranking out content *like it's their job*! Is it any wonder why I recognize all my ideas in their stuff?

It's because my generation of wand-waving, lightsaber-swinging, cursed-Aztec gold-burying kids are grown up now, and we're all trying to write stories inspired by the same content. When I watch a show or read the latest best-selling fantasy series, I very quickly come to the realization that some other person had the idea first because, guess what, that person also grew up on the same stories that inspired the same idea which, only moments ago, I thought was divinely inspired.

Alright. There's my dramatic beginning. To be sure, all the above is slapdash conjecture. I can't prove any of it. However, it is the narrative that runs in my head. And I guess that's what I actually want to talk about. How do we get over these invisible and probably untrue mental hurdles that come with writing fiction in a world that seems to be drowning in it? (And, by the way, not necessarily bad fiction. If you got the idea that I sit back and scoff at all the content because it's bad and overdone, then let me clarify: some of it is bad, sure, but so much of it is wildly good. This, by the way, can also feel defeating. Now I'm certain I have nothing to contribute!)

I'm inspired by guys like C.S. Lewis and J.R.R. Tolkien (both of whom, surprise, surprise, inspire a billion other people. My point exactly! Another teary peanut M&M). Anyway, I like those guys because they saw the value of telling stories in a culture that valued, above all, the rational, cold, hard fact. In a world of sterile, lab coat-thinking, Tolkien and Lewis saw it as a noble endeavor to talk about elves and fawns. Magical worlds, threatening villains… they believed it was good work to talk of such things because woven into the fabric of those tales was the truth, like deep stuff just as good, if not better, than the stuff you get in a lab. Real truth, just sitting there for the taking for anyone willing to read and use their imaginations. Storytelling was brave. It was necessary. Who wouldn't be inspired?

But if I'm honest, I inhabit a totally different world from them. We are not in the clinical modern era. Ours is quite colorful, one where people spend more time watching Netflix and discussing the latest HBO mini-series than they do the news. At least in my experience, fiction is no longer the rare and brave path to find truth (I know, I know, it still is that, hence my dream to write stories, but catch my drift), fiction is the broad road we're all marching on every evening after the kids are in bed.

Again, let's clarify: I don't think this is a bad thing. Mine is an imaginative generation, and so is the one below me. We've been shaped and molded by stories that are strange and new, fantastical and mind-bending. We dream because we feast on the ingredients of dreams. But when I set out to contribute, I can't help but feel overwhelmed, doubting if there is a place for a young, budding fiction author out there.

And yet, here I am, just weeks away from typing the words "the end" on my Very. First. Book. And now, only as I look back, do I see that I have climbed over some of those mental hurdles.

As I approach the final stages of writing this story—one with fantastical settings, magic, and a cosmic battle of good and evil like so many others—I realize that somewhere along the way, the sharp bite of doubt that comes from watching and reading a lot of fiction has, over time, faded. I have decided that writing fiction is less like binging peanut M&M's, and more like making a casserole for a potluck, one with a long guest list of hungry friends and family. Is there really space for another casserole? YES!

In place of all the doubt, lately, I've been pondering a new thing: I wonder how many other fiction authors out there stop halfway through the journey because they have the same experience as me. They're convinced they've struck gold with an idea, but then they find themselves reading a similar iteration of that very idea in the latest novel they picked up at Barnes & Noble, and by the end of the day, they've given up.

If that's you, I feel ya (see lament above). That was me. Some days that *is* me. But as I've thought about my own journey in finally getting this story out of my head and onto paper, I've collected three, tidy little nuggets of encouragement to keep in mind if you find yourself doubting whether or not your story can be baked into something edible for the potluck. I've kept them in the back of my mind, and, you know what, here we are! I'm almost done with my first novel and, as far as I know, there isn't another Jace Schwartz out there who has written the exact same thing. I've produced a new and original thing! Sure, my casserole has corn and cheese and sour cream. After all, it's inspired by the great potlucks of our time. But it is new, nonetheless. This brings me to my first thought.

#1: Everyone is inspired by something.

I don't know who said this first. I'm sure some genius somewhere wrote it down on parchment with a feathered quill (if that's you, forgive my lack of citation). In any case, a trusted brother of mine said it, almost in passing. He's a creative genius himself, and it struck me how unbothered he was by the idea of inspiration. You can get hung up on the fact that we're all, at some point in life, inspired by the epic journey through Middle-earth, or you can appreciate it, even enjoy it, and get on with what you have to say about it (speaking of which, we should also note that Tolkien himself, and Lewis, and good old George Lucas, were all drawing on content of their own too, even if it looks like they pulled their ideas out of thin air!).

Every church lady with the best cheesy potatoes was inspired by another church lady with cheesy potatoes.

So, perhaps we all grew up with *Star Wars* as kids, but we all took different paths as adults, and though the seeds of inspiration look the same for many of us, the truth is, depending on the environmental conditions of where those seeds grow, there can be great variety to the trees that sprout up. So, if you have a sneaking suspicion that you and that author you're reading are both inspired by the same stuff, smile and remember that everyone is inspired by something, and if you're waiting for sheer originality to come at the beginning of a piece of art, it will never arrive. Originality always comes at the back end, once you've finished the project and realize, as you step back, that you have, in fact, created something new.

#2: Characters showcase originality more than anything else.

Again, someone authoritative probably said this, and I'm sure with some Googling I could probably find out who, exactly, posited it for the first time. To that sage, whoever you are, I thank you. Personally, though, I first heard this from, again, another friend of mine. He read my first few chapters, heard me moan about all that I've been moaning and griping to you all about, then said simply: "Yeah, I think I've been in a version of your world before. I've definitely been aboard a ship before. I've been in a castle before. I've seen magic before. And I've met villains and heroes before. But you know what, I've never met this character before, and I'm intrigued."

Our reckless, binging diet of Netflix tells me two things. 1) It tells me that we're spoiled for content and probably have too much of it. But also, it tells me 2) We never get tired of new characters and the stories they inhabit. Your concepts might be a bit recycled, same with your settings, and even your plot (I mean let's be honest, in most of these stories, good is going to defeat evil and the protagonist will overcome the odds), but when you put all the ingredients together in whatever combination you're working on and then put a character right smack dab in the middle, something amazing always happens! You'll step back at the end of a chapter and say, "Wow, I see a lot of my inspirational sources in this chapter, but fundamentally, I've never read this before. My character is coming alive. This. Is. New."

#3: Creating is harder than critiquing

Right around the time when the whole world got weirdly obsessed with *Game of Thrones*, I noticed an intense spike in narrative critique. Suddenly, a billion people became experts on what it means to tell a good story and how the writers for the *Game of Thrones* television series were ruining it.

There's enough controversy surrounding *Game of Thrones* that I'll happily refrain from weighing in on whether the critiques were valid. Frankly, I'm unqualified, and it is neither here nor there for me. What I will say, however, is that the spike in Rotten-Tomato-style reviews coming from everyone and their dog revealed one thing very clearly: it takes much more energy to create than it does to critique, and we're all very good at slipping easily into the latter without ever dipping our toes in the former.

The truth is if you have an idea for a story, and you're like me, needlessly worried about all the stuff out there that looks like your stuff, or whether or not you're original, or whether or not it'll be received well (especially in light of how critical the internet-peanut-gallery can be), just remember that you could very easily become someone who consumes and critiques but never, ever contributes. It can be scary to contribute to a world addicted to outrage. But discipline yourself to keep writing, to keep going, knowing that this world needs more creative contributors and fewer consumers. We need more innovative ideas, and while you might fear your idea is not one of those, the truth is, once you've worked hard to see a piece of art all the way through to its full creation, you have, every time, produced something that wasn't there five minutes ago. And that's very encouraging. It might not change the world, but I promise you that every idea that does change the world has something in common with yours: that person decided to create, not just critique.

So, start throwing cheese and potatoes into a dish and see what happens, kids. Sure, there will be others making something similar. After all, we're all inspired by George Lucas's cheesy chicken and broccoli masterpiece. But that doesn't mean we're making the same stuff. There's always room for more casserole at the potluck! And, come on, you don't want to be the guy who shows up to the potluck empty-handed anyway. Eat, enjoy, and contribute! We have many, many more stories to tell.

At the Table of Misfits
by Rachael Mitchell

I walked up the front steps of my new-to-me junior high, zipping closed my thin windbreaker, no match against the biting Minnesota March wind. In the front office, I nervously waited for the student who was assigned to show me to each of my classes. When she arrived to pick me up, I was struck by our obvious differences in attire. I made mental notes about her oversized hair bow and preppy rugby shirt, wondering if my casual oversized jeans and sweatshirt—considered cool from the small town I came from—would fit in or stick out.

Walking down the hall together, she seemed to know everyone, yet introduced me to no one. I remained on the outskirts of her conversations as she showed me to my first class. When the bell rang after first period, I waited for a few minutes in the hall for her, as the school counselor had made it clear she'd show me to each class throughout the day. As the halls began to clear out and there was no sign of her, I had to make it to my second class on my own, yet I had no idea where it was. Walking slowly down the hall, as students filed past and into their classrooms, the room numbers were getting bigger, and I realized I was going the wrong way. *Brrrrrriiiiinnnnnnnggg!* The bell rang loudly in the empty hall and in my ears. There I was, tardy to my second-period class on my first day of school in a state I had moved to three days before. I finally found the right room, opened the door, and twenty-four sets of eyes watched me find an empty desk near the back of the room.

As the day went on, I slowly got better at finding my way around, and eventually, it was time for lunch. I followed the drone of chaotic noise until it grew louder and found the cafeteria. Having enrolled this late in the school year, there was already a clear order and routine to the lunch procedure, and I was learning on the fly. I scanned the room quickly, thankfully spotting the oversized bow on the head of my no-show tour guide. Though I didn't want to sit by her, she was the only familiar face I recognized, and there was an empty seat across from her. I sat, relieved to not be standing and sticking out like a sore thumb above the crowd of heads. Just as I was opening my lunch bag, there was a tap on my shoulder. A girl, presumably an unhelpful friend of my unhelpful acquaintance, looked down at me and said, "Um…that's my seat." When I realized she was serious and wanted me to move, I stuffed my sandwich back into my lunch bag in disbelief and took a walk of shame to the table of obvious outcasts where I sat each day until the school year finally, mercifully ended a few months later.

This traumatic move in middle school emphasized how unknown I really was. Though it was the first time I felt exposed, it wasn't the last time I'd feel vulnerable. Fast forward a couple of decades to today. As a first-time author, I naively thought if I put in the work to write a book, I would be rewarded with a publishing deal. However, just like in middle school, I'm once again on the outside looking in, seated at the outcast table. A decade ago, the unknown author's ticket to building a platform was writing a book. A well-written book, with representation, got published. With their publishing deal, the writer established themselves as an author and became known to their readers, the readers demanded more, and the author got more book deals. But in the age of social media, publishing has shifted to offering book deals to those who already have an established following. A well-written book is no longer the ticket to building a platform. A large social media following is now the ticket to securing a publishing deal.

Even with two out of the three ingredients: a well-written book and representation, the third ingredient—being unknown on social media—has prevented my book from going to publication. One after one, the rejections from publishers rolled in, "It's a wonderful concept, and there was a lot to love about the proposal, but alas, our marketing and publicity folks had too many reservations about the platform," followed by, "Unfortunately we've decided not to pursue this project, I don't think this one will work well in our list without an author platform." After a couple dozen similar responses, my reality crystallized: I'm an unknown author unworthy of being published because of my small social media following.

So here I sit in a loud cafeteria of authors. The cool table is a few tables away. I recognize the authors at that table. I read their books, watch them on social media, and see them get mass distribution deals with Target. They get six-figure advances and offers to write multiple books. Watching them succeed, I'm reminded of middle school in Minnesota and the no-show tour guide with the oversized bow. These authors are the popular, cool kids.

Meanwhile, I'm over here at the misfit table. At first, I'm embarrassed to be counted among the outcasts. At this table sits the awkward and unusual, and I think to myself, "Surely, I'm in the wrong seat, these cannot be my people, I belong at the cool table." And just as I start to excuse myself from this table of misfits, a welcoming voice says, "Here, come sit by me." A kind smile and a hand eagerly patting a seat intrigues me. I glance at the no-seats-left cool table, watching people clamber for space, and back to the misfits. The choice is laid before me, should I quit because it feels unfair or shall I discover the beauty of what's right in front of me? This experiment may not be polished or perfect. I probably won't resonate with each person or every story, but my favorite quote—*Do not despise these small beginnings*—rings through my ears as I swallow my pride, and take a seat.

I soon discover I'm welcome and accepted here. I slowly learn the stories and passions of the other unknown authors at the table, and they hear mine. These are my people. Over time, our table gets louder as we cheer each other on. Friendships deepen, and real stories of life's heartache and triumphs are shared. We care authentically, not looking for stories masked as new, fresh content. We don't have reputations or brands to maintain. We don't have to partner, create giveaways, or link to Amazon. We can fail without the fear of being canceled; we can love without the pressure of happy endings.

It was time for action. I look around the table of misfits, united by our continued state of being unknown. Instead of adding more chairs to the fringe of the cool table, my friends and I build our own table. This new table functions independently of the approval, support, and dysfunction of the table we used to long to be a part of.

The Unknown Authors Club was born, at first out of fury, but then from the desire to re-create what seems well-established and create a seat at the table for everyone. My two friends and I became the tour guides that show up. We don't ditch brand-new writers wandering in the halls of trying to get published. We welcome without reservation or critique. We cheer on and promote other writers trying to find their way. We amplify stories and voices worthy of being heard.

It doesn't feel like what I thought being at the cool table would feel like. There are fewer freebies, TV appearances, and less money over here, but there is more celebration, authenticity, and discovery. Building a table I never wanted to sit at has brought me more joy than I ever expected, and this misfit can't imagine sitting anywhere else.

Acknowledgments

For me, trying to get my words into the world has felt a little like wandering in the desert for 40 years—long, hot, lonely, and though my sandals have never worn out, my oh my, how tired I am of manna! And then, like the moving of the cloud, about a year and a half ago I saw an Instagram post from Joy Eggerichs Reed that changed the trajectory of my journey. I would like to thank her for her fun and slightly aggressive efforts to help authors, known and unknown, as they embark on the publishing journey. I would also like to thank my dear internet-turned-real life friends, Rachael and Leslee, from whom I have received incredible encouragement along the way, and with whom I have discovered a new enthusiasm and optimism about our mutual writing future. We've done our part, ladies, so as we step into this new Jordan, I can't wait to see what God has planned! Finally, thank you to my parents who have always been my biggest cheerleaders, and to my husband who, though he joined the squad later in life, has more than made up for it with his radical and ridiculously overestimated view of my talents.

— *Jodi Cowles*

* * *

Thank you to all the publishers and editors who have rejected my work. Your rejections fueled my fire and propelled me forward in steely determination to neither give up nor pander to the masses on TikTok. You've made me more determined to steadily be myself, to be ok with small beginnings, and to find a third way, even if I had to do it myself. Which I didn't. Because the solution was rooted in community.

Jodi and Leslee, from the tiny spark that fanned into a blaze taking down the regime *Les Mis* style, to us actualizing a dream, each step has been exponentially more fun, more rewarding, and more inspiring than if we each had done it alone. To my "extra" and "loading" friends, thank you for being all that and even a smidge more.

Thank you Joy for rewarding me with the best "yes" and allowing me to be a part of your first cohort. Though I was expecting to instantly turn my work into a million-dollar book deal with merch and a movie, I've gained something more valuable: friendship.

Thank you Neal, Hollis, Ryder, and Dane for your encouragement and patience while I've been in meetings, and thank you to Tim and Joy, Jon, Rinner, and Camden for being able to fend for yourselves when the UAC was on a roll.

— *Rachael Mitchell*

* * *

To the MarcoPolo video messaging app — This book, this friendship, heck, even this dream of publishing wouldn't have happened without you. You were there from the very beginning when Jodi, Rachael, and I met in Joy Eggerichs Reed's book writing cohort in March 2021. I am certain Joy would appreciate it if I acknowledged her role in bringing the three of us together—which, technically she did—but it was you, MarcoPolo, who made our relationship thrive. You have continued to be a bright spot in an otherwise dull social media world, and have made planning our world domination of publishing unknown authors possible across three time zones and two continents. You are worth every penny of the $59.99 annual subscription I pay for your

"Plus" membership. I would pay that and more if you promise to never get rid of your playback speed option. Listening to my business partners and friends at 1.5x speed is the gift that keeps on giving, and helps me help them to get to the point much, much faster.

To Jodi & Rachael — Your friendship and loyalty are equal to your savviness and snark, all qualities I highly admire in people I want to do life with, let alone go into business with. Thank you for saying yes to this crazy idea and for tolerating my bossiness along the way. To pay for my task-master tendencies, I promise to make ridiculous Instagram Reels with you anytime you want. With Rachael directing and Jodi serving as the props master, I know I'm in good hands. You are the best partners to jump into the unknown with, and I can't wait to see where this experiment takes us.

To our Unknown Authors — Thank you for saying yes and taking a chance on three unknown authors to publish your words. Your belief in this project has been the tide that lifted our spirits and kept us afloat while we sailed toward publishing for the very first time. We are honored to print your words in this book and look forward to featuring you, and many other unknown authors, in future publications. Together we rise.

To my family — Thank you for supporting me in making this book a reality. I apologize for the many, many nights I was still working and dinner wasn't made, let alone even thought about. I know that food is your love language, so your ability to conjure up a sandwich or bring me Chick-fil-A meant a lot. I will get back to the kitchen eventually, I promise. I also realize that I probably sounded a bit like Charlie Brown's teacher with my *wha-wha-wha-wha*'s when explaining what this book was all about. Thank you for nodding your head in agreement and being proud of me even if you weren't 100 percent sure what I was doing. That's what family does—support one another even when we don't always understand why. You have been a shining example of this and for that, I am forever grateful. I love you.

— *Leslee Stewart*

About the Contributors

CINDY ARNOLD is a math teacher and preacher. Despite childhood dreams of teaching high school English and a degree to back it up, Cindy has taught various levels of high school math (except geometry, thank goodness) since 2007. Cindy's 1,500 former students insist her English major is being put to good use, though, as she talks more than any other math teacher they have ever had. After leading small group discussions and collaborating on a new church plant, in 2016 Cindy started preaching as a lay speaker in her home church. She now preaches often throughout her area as a Certified Lay Speaker of the United Methodist Church and continues to teach math at the Algebra I level. Cindy currently lives in Springfield, IL, with her cat, Tillie, and enjoys reading, spoiling her nephew, James, gardening, crocheting, and hiking. Follow Cindy's writing at @mathteacherpreacher on Instagram.

JJ BARROWS is a comedian, author, and mixed media artist who's performed in comedy clubs, churches, and awkward dinner parties all over America. However, don't assume colorful and comedic means a lack of honesty. JJ has also traversed the difficulties of eating disorders, family dysfunctions, and an on-and-off struggle with depression. With a refreshing storyteller style, she reveals the freedom a quippy sense of humor can reveal in all of us by giving breath to those gritty moments. She released a Dry Bar Comedy Special, published her first book, *it's called a spade*, and wrote, produced, and starred in her own comedy special filmed on location at home…all thanks to COVID clearing her schedule and freeing up all her time. Her favorite career highlight was meeting Rob Lowe in a parking lot, until most recently when Dolly Parton waved to her and she momentarily forgot to keep breathing. When she's not performing, painting, or trying to find her way back to the ocean, she's introverting at home in Tennessee with her husband, Josh Newton. You can find her on Instagram @jjbarrows, as well as watch her videos, shop her art, and sign up for her email list at jjbarrows.com.

ROSE BOOTH hails from Louisville, Kentucky, where she was born and raised. As an only child to older parents, she was encouraged to be an independent soul. This has served her well as a single, never-married woman living to serve Christ. Rose has worked for more than thirty years in the technology and publishing space. She received her MBA in 2015 and thrives in environments where she can mentor and counsel others to grow in their careers and personal lives. Rose co-directs the women's ministry at her church and also co-teaches her ladies' Bible study class. Her passion in ministry is teaching and discipleship, and she loves working with women of college age and above. Becoming an amputee in December 2021 has caused Rose to see life from a different perspective as she learns to navigate this new normal. Rose co-hosts the podcast, One Single Thought, with her friend, Heather Bump. When she's not writing, Rose loves to spend time with friends, craft, and read. She also loves shocking people with the news that she is a distant relative of John Wilkes Booth. You can keep up with Rose through her website, rosebooth.net or on Instagram @RosieBoo65.

JODI COWLES is an author and a recovering expat. After working in a cubicle for a decade, Jodi was propelled to visit more than 45 countries, taking up residence in seven. From teaching English to non-profit video production, her work expanded her vision for the world and allowed her to collect stories along the way. Armed with an endless supply of culture-clashing mishaps, inappropriate marriage proposals, and language barrier misfires, Jodi's writing gets to the heart of the matter: the human connection present in every country and culture. She and her husband have a young daughter, and most recently ran a business teaching English in Istanbul,

Turkey. You can follow Jodi and her author adventures at jodicowles.com or on Instagram @jodicowles.

KAREN deBLIECK is still a teenager even though she's spent 40-something years on this earth. She stays up way too late reading books under the covers and eats far too much pizza. Living in the great Canadian north with her husband and four young adults she does not, in fact, like the cold or snow. Her books are laced with a history that wasn't taught in school, and teenage love, antics, and pain that transcends time. She's a firm believer that people's hearts open to change when they hear the words, "Once Upon a Time." Her writing has won awards from The Word Guild (Canada) and ACFW. More recently she received a BIPOC scholarship to both the SCBWI Winter and Summer conference. Her writing reflects the tensions of racial identity and belonging that she struggled with as a black teen adopted by a white family. She began writing as a teen to understand her feelings and the world around her. It started with angsty poetry and evolved into short stories and novels. Her dream is to share her characters and stories with the world, especially those who feel like they're living in-between two worlds. Although she's currently an unknown author she's enjoying writing and spending time with others who enjoy books as much as she does. You can read more of Karen's writing at karendeblieck.com or follow her on Instagram @deblieckkaren.

JOY EGGERICHS REED is the founder of Punchline Agency: a literary and speaking agency for people good on the page and stage. Aside from managing and negotiating on behalf of authors and speakers, Joy consults with aspiring writers, speakers, and those seeking to clarify a message or idea. Prior to being an agent, Joy got her start as a blogger and speaker, creating over 500 written and video posts and speaking to audiences of up to 12,000 people on the topic of singleness and relationships. In 2017, Joy launched Punchline Agency to represent and develop communicators and voices she believed needed to be heard. She currently resides as an expat in Paris, France with her husband

Matt and two petite bébés, Millie and Emerson. Collectively, their family consumes thirty-four percent of the country's croissant production. For more about Punchline Agency, visit punchlineagency.com. Joy loves to share about her adventures in Paris and publishing on Instagram @joyeggerichs.

MAREN HEIBERG is originally from Minnesota, but has lived in Darjeeling, India for 15 years. In Darjeeling, she met her husband and they have been married for 10 years. Maren and her husband have a seven-year-old son and a four-year-old daughter. Maren graduated from Hope College in Michigan with a degree in Literature. She has been writing for years but published her first two books in 2020 during the pandemic. *The Adventures of Pandi the Panda* and *Ajay's COVID Questions* were both written for the children of Darjeeling where she lives. She dreams of writing more books both for children and adults in the future. You can follow her writing adventures on Instagram @havenfreelance.

BETHANY McMILLON is a coffee, football, and ice cream lover from Texas. She adores her number-loving accountant husband and her growing too-fast boy. Bethany loves her work as an elementary school assistant principal. She is passionate about building deeper relationships with both Jesus and those that she loves. Her spirit is most settled after she has connected with a friend about God's mercy and grace over coffee, sweet tea on the patio, or even a side-by-side walk through a local neighborhood. She hopes to encourage women to find and hold onto those connections within busy and quick-paced lives. Bethany writes occasionally on her website, BethanyMcMillon.com. She can also be found on Instagram @BethanyMcMillon.

RACHAEL MITCHELL is a writer and speaker, wife and mom, who relies on faith, humor and an up-to-date Google calendar to make it through. There's a high chance you'll catch Rachael dressed in sweatpants with a book in one hand, a cup of tea in the other, totally forgetting that she's supposed to be in the car picking up a kid from soccer practice. Though she majored in English, was a paid product copywriter for two large national retailers, and dabbled in small writing projects here and there, she didn't accept the title as writer until she launched Mitchell Freelance in 2020. Her copywriting business provides well-known and mom-and-pop companies with strong, but clear and concise, copy. Rachael enjoys the beach, camping, connecting with friends and family, and resides in Issaquah, WA. You can follow her writing adventures on Instagram @mitchellfreelancewriting.

TANYA MOTORIN is a first-time author who always thought she had a book in her but didn't know what to write about. That changed when she was diagnosed with breast cancer in July of 2018, and she knew that her first book would be about her breast cancer journey. As a breast cancer survivor, her hope is that through vulnerability and sharing her personal experience in her book, *Covered: My Breast Cancer Journey and Practical Insight for Yours*, she will encourage and help other women feel known, cared for, and resourced as they walk through their own journeys with breast cancer. Tanya has been on staff full-time with Athletes in Action, an international Christian sports ministry since 2002, and she and her husband are currently serving the athletic community at UCLA and the LA coastline. She loves spending time writing, creating, organizing, cooking, buying more than she needs at Target, and getting some self-care by going on a run or a long walk. Tanya also loves spending time with friends and family, traveling, going to the beach, camping, hiking, laughing hard, and watching a good movie. She and her husband Nikita live in Mar Vista, California with their daughters Hope and Sophia, their son, Zion, their Chiweenie, Daisy, and their hamster, Seymour. You can follow Tanya on Instagram @tvlasagna or read more of her work at tanyamotorin.com.

DANI NICHOLS is a writer, cowgirl, and mom of three from Central Oregon.She writes about adoption, family, horses, faith, and above all, the relentless nature of redemption. Her debut book for children, *Buzz the Not-So-Brave*, about her quirky and skittish quarter horse, was released in summer 2022. Her work has won several writing contests and been published in Fathom Magazine, Oregon Humanities, Fallow Ink, and others, as well as several anthologies. To read more from Dani, check out her website and newsletter at wranglerdani.com and @buzzthenotsobrave on Instagram.

DON PAPE is a book lover but, more importantly, loves to discover and support unknown authors. After 35 years on the editorial side of the publishing industry, he is now a literary agent, working with writers from around the globe who are yet to be discovered through his agency, Pape Commons. With a stubborn streak, he has a penchant for representing the underdog and those less interested in memes, and more concerned about prepositions and good grammar. He is married to his best friend, Ruthie, has three sons, two amazing daughters-in-law, and Zoey and Ozzie, his amazingly talented granddaughters. You can find out more about his agency at papecommons.com.

BLAKNI RILEY is well acquainted with the one, two sucker punches called grief and loss. Yanked unwillingly into the ring after yet another death, she was confronted with her beliefs about Christ. Was He really who she had professed Him to be with her mouth? With nothing left to lose, she called Him a liar and practically dared Him to strike her dead. In that moment, she would have welcomed it to her pain. Fully agreeing with Job's wife, a barrage of thoughts and repressed questions bled out. Was He really who He said He was? Could she trust Him? Answers chalked full of YES resulted in a calling to pursue, encourage, reconcile, and restore wounded hearts to the freedom only found in the faithfulness of Christ. She shares her writing on Instagram @blakniriley.

JACE SCHWARTZ lives in Vancouver, WA, with his wife and two small children. They can usually be spotted in their humble backyard, enjoying afternoon tea together, or hurrying out the door with a half-zipped diaper bag flung over the shoulder, late for church, or a family gathering. Depending on the day and the weather, Schwartz's wardrobe changes from that of a college professor, to pastor, to student, to writer, to wanna-be gardener. If you're interested in journeying along with Jace as he debuts his first book, sign up for his newsletter: http://eepurl.com/h3szHb.

LESLEE STEWART is an author and speaker who loves to share a little bit about a lot of things and a lot about the One thing that matters. Over the years, she's worn many different titles: reporter, communications executive, ministry leader, and that one time when she stepped up to the plate and volunteered to be her son's little league coach. While each role came with varying levels of success, her life experiences continue to make great material for highly-relatable storytelling. Married to her husband Jon for 25 years, her favorite role is that of sideline cheerleader for her two, sports-obsessed teenage sons. Her goals in life are simple—learning to master the perfect guacamole, getting her boys to appreciate musicals, and someday singing backup for Aretha Franklin in heaven. Follow Leslee's writing at lesleestewart.substack.com or on Instagram @lesleeystewart.

SAMANTHA STEWART is an Okie who has never lived outside of her buckle of the Bible Belt. She loves country music and walking barefoot whenever she can. Samantha had never considered writing or even calling herself a writer until the summer of 2021 when her husband passed away. She began her writing career by journaling about all things medical, but her writing became public and more consistent when she started her blog, Reveal the Wonders. Her journey of grief, widowhood, and all that God is calling her to do and say is unfolding in front of her readers. Samantha has been an educator for 25 years. When not at school, Samantha loves to experience life by jumping out of planes, getting a new tattoo, taking road trips to places yet to be explored, or relaxing at home with her daughter and English bulldog, Willa Dean. You can follow Samantha on Instagram @revealthewonders and her website, revealthewonders.com.

About The Unknown Authors Club

THE UNKNOWN AUTHORS CLUB was formed by Jodi Cowles, Rachael Mitchell, and Leslee Stewart—three aspiring authors who met in a writing cohort in March 2021. Each arrived at the cohort with a book in their heart and a dream of being courted by a publisher who would bring their book ideas to life. But those dreams were quickly dashed after each submitted their proposals and received a chorus of resounding "no's" from publishers. The problem wasn't their content—these three could definitely write! The problem was nobody knew who they were. No publisher would take a chance on a writer who didn't have a built-in audience of tens of thousands of potential readers.

Disappointed but determined, these three set out to find a new way to help authors like themselves get published, even if they're not currently trending on TikTok. Together, they created a social community and publishing platform designed to celebrate unknown authors regardless of their influencer status.

Their first publication, *The Life of an Unknown Author: an Anthology on Writing and Publishing from the Best Authors You Haven't Yet Read* features essays from the three founders, as well as fellow unknown authors, all focused on the topic of what it means to be unknown. By capitalizing on the micro-communities of the multiple authors featured in the anthology, their publication has the potential to reach more than 50,000 readers. How's that for being unknown?

To find out more, visit www.theunknownauthorsclub.com or follow their adventures on Instagram @theunknownauthorsclub.

Made in United States
North Haven, CT
11 October 2022

25321533R00065